MAKING THE HUMAN MIND

R.A.Sharpe

London and New York

First published 1990
by Routledge
11 New Fetter Lane, London EC4P 4EE

Simultaneously published in the USA and Canada
by Routledge
a division of Routledge, Chapman and Hall, Inc.
29 West 35th Street, New York, NY 10001

Typeset in 10/12 Garamond by
Columns of Reading
Printed in Great Britain by
T J Press (Padstow) Ltd, Padstow, Cornwall

British Library Cataloguing in Publication Data
Sharpe, R. A.
Making the human mind.
1. Mind − Philosophical perspectives
I. Title
128′.2

Library of Congress Cataloging in Publication Data
Sharpe, R. A.
Making the human mind / R.A. Sharpe
p.   cm.
Includes bibliographical references.
1. Philosophy of mind. I. Title.
BD418.3.S5 1990
128′.2—dc20
ISBN 0−415−04767−6

CONTENTS

PREFACE

I had nearly finished this book when I discovered the text on which it might be a sermon: 'But with a human being the assumption is that it is impossible to gain an insight into the mechanism. Thus indeterminacy is postulated' (Wittgenstein, *Remarks on the Philosophy of Psychology*, 666).

The position I adopt is more extreme than this since I am advocating a form of anti-realism with respect to the mental; in the course of this enquiry we encounter some chestnuts such as freedom, akrasia and the holistic nature of mental concepts. Intellectual debts will to some extent be obvious; they are primarily Davidson and Wittgenstein, the former because he is wrong about many of the major issues I discuss and a good deal of argument is directed against a worthy opponent. If Davidson did not exist I should have had to invent him. The influence of Wittgenstein was at first mediated through the influence of David Cockburn and Lars Hertzberg, who read the book in its entirety, and then through, in particular, the second volume of the *Remarks on the Philosophy of Psychology*. The debt is sufficiently pervasive to make detailed reference otiose. Dummett is the *éminence grise*. The MS was extensively revised during a spell at Abo Akademi in Finland and a series of seminars on the text at Helsinki and elsewhere in Scandinavia were beyond price. Finally I dedicate this to Pam whose interest in the social sciences over the years was a spur.

Parts have appeared elsewhere, chapter three as an article in *Inquiry*, 1988, parts of chapter two as a contribution to a Habermas symposium and other parts of this chapter as an inaugural lecture. A version of chapter four appeared as 'Prudence and akrasia' in J. Srednicki (ed.), *Philosophical Contributions*, S. Korner, Nijhoff, 1987.

vii

INTRODUCTION

Let me begin with an evolutionary fable, one which I will develop further in the last chapter. Our remote ancestors were ape-like hominids. But they could predict what others wanted and intended. My pet cat can do as much. She can tell whether I am going to sit in an easy chair where she can sit on my lap or whether I am going into the garden. She has beliefs about what I will do. If mammals with less complex patterns of behaviour can predict what another mammal will do then evidently one hominid could tell to some extent what another would do. Like my cat their behaviour incorporates the beliefs which they have about their fellows. I shall say more about 'incorporates' in chapter three. For the moment consider that if a mammal displays fear then another mammal can predict what it would do if attacked. Furthermore we can say that the fear involves the belief that the animal is in some way threatened. We can say this without wanting to say that the animal is able to describe the object of its own fear. There is no problem about accrediting complex mammals with beliefs as displayed in their actions.

Of course, once I have language what I can recognise in others I can describe in them and what I can describe in them I will soon describe of myself. I can recognise my intentions in my behaviour just as others can. What I shall argue in the final chapter is that thoughts become possible if we have language to describe the beliefs implicit in action. Our conscious beliefs are prompted first by our seeing them in other's actions and then by our describing them, first in others, then in ourselves.

If this sketch is accurate, what sort of angle does it give us on realism? If realism insists that matters of fact exist independently of our thinking them and that, *a fortiori*, this is true of beliefs then

1

my account is non-realist in some respects since to have conscious beliefs depends upon our being able to attribute beliefs (though the dependence is causal). Beliefs as continuants or occurrents as opposed to those beliefs incorporated in action exist because we think them. Conscious beliefs are, in this respect, constructions. They are similar to what a non-realist in mathematics believes numbers to be. They exist because we attempt to understand the actions of others. We see these beliefs in the actions of others and create them in ourselves once we have a language. Once beliefs can be so internalised they can be formulated antecedent to action rather than *post hoc*.

Some of these beliefs are truths about us. It is a matter of fact that I believe that Wales is part of the United Kingdom and somebody else's belief that I have this belief is true. The world is that way. In that sense realism holds. But many of our beliefs about others may well be undetermined by the facts to which they relate. The facts, then, are occasions for interpretation. Certainly it may be unequivocally true that a child is angry. But there are many cases where there is no fact of the matter and we err if we think that it is simply lack of knowledge which forbids us the truth.

In the course of this book I make many assumptions about the mind and our way of talking about it. I do not much like talking of 'the mind' since it invites a spurious contrast with 'the physical' but in setting up a philosophical theory one is the victim of one's predecessors and there may be no intelligible alternative to introducing my views in this way. I assume, for a start, that when we talk about our emotions and other forms of mental activity such as cogitation, our concepts are not highly inconsistent. It is impossible to learn or communicate unless the elements of our talk are mainly coherent. Indeed any understanding which presumed that they were in irredeemable conflict would be hardly competent as a translation. It is, however, to my mind a possibility that at a more abstract level our talk might involve incoherences which are the result of contrasting pressures which come to bear upon our conceptual scheme. Political, religious, philosophical or societal influences may cause us to develop a system of ideas which is incoherent just because our interests and desires conflict. Ideologies exhibit this tendency. The penultimate chapter of this book debates such issues.

I also assume that there is a dynamic relation between concepts.

They serve purposes and may be so arranged as to protect certain fundamental assumptions, say about realism or objectivity. I assume that something analagous to natural selection has led to the concepts we have behaving as they do. There are many instances in this book where I suggest that specific criteria of assertability develop because of certain pressures which come from our interests. The way a form of ersatz determinacy develops is one such and both here and in some of my other writings I have paid attention to this. I make a deal of what I call 'surrogate realism'. This is an ersatz form of realism where we create a means of settling questions so that we can say of a statement that it is true or false even though there are no independent facts to which these assertions correspond or fail to correspond.

The final chapter completes the argument of the book in maintaining that the human conscious mind is itself a human creation, brought about through linguistic behaviour. It is a by-product of human action. It is thus unsurprising that human beings should be appropriate objects for the sort of hermeneutics which characterises the way we comprehend the other creations of human kind, our art, our history, our institutions, our culture and practices. And so the arch of the argument is completed by this keystone. We created our minds. They are our artefacts brought about by the development of language. Contrary to Emerson's thesis, consciousness (or at least self consciousness) is the gift of language.

Now read on.

1

THE PARATACTIC IMAGINATION

. . . so, o'er that art
  Which you say adds to nature, is an art
That nature makes. You see, sweet maid, we marry
  A gentler scion to the wildest stock,
  And make conceive a bark of baser kind
By bud of nobler race. This is an art
  Which does mend nature, change it rather, but
The art itself is nature.

The Winter's Tale, IV, III

I

This book has a number of interrelated themes. One dominant theme is anticipated in the quotation from *The Winter's Tale* which provides my epigraph. It is the contrast between nature and human agency. One aim is to give a general account of the understanding of human actions and creations which contrasts with the forms of explanation proper to the natural sciences. I follow the hermeneutic tradition which takes the study of man to require a form of understanding distinct from the explanation of physical events. In this I join forces with writers as diverse as Dilthey and Gadamer on the one hand and Winch on the other. But there is another aspect of the contrast between nature and art embodied in Polixenes's speech and it is the way in which nature itself makes art. The initial phrase 'an art that nature makes' is ambiguous, though that ambiguity is ultimately resolved. Does art make the nature or is it nature that makes art? There could be an art, more fundamental than that which adds to nature, which makes it. So the question I try to answer in this book may be phrased: what is the nature of man such that he is necessarily not only a creature who makes things for interpretation, but who, in making his own nature, makes himself a creature to be interpreted rather than to be explained? Thus the suggestion is that our nature is, at least in part, a consequence of our own activity and hence needs to be placed beside the creations of mankind such as our arts, our history and our societies. It has been said that Nietzsche paid man the highest compliment when he said that he created himself.

The understanding of persons and of their creations, I shall argue, is very different from the understanding of natural processes and physical objects, the targets of scientific enquiry. But positivism, the idea that natural science offers the paradigm for human enquiry, is so prevalent that even where we pay no lip service to physics and its cousins, the model of science pervades. My principal task in this book is to give an account of the hermeneutic approach to man and his products which will show how characteristic features of man which seem to require a 'hidden mechanism' type of explanation can be explained in other ways. Weakness of will and self deception are perhaps the most important such features. They seem to require an understanding in terms of sub-agents much as the germ theory of disease explains macro symptoms in terms of micro agents. What I shall argue is that a model of interpretation taken from the arts can, with suitable modifications, account for the varieties of such areas of human enquiry as psychology, history, sociology and the arts. Inevitably a by-product of this is a conception of what man is.

In an idealist era in philosophy, the arts are likely to become an important model for philosophical enquiry and method. Concepts at home in aesthetics will be applied elsewhere; a good example is Dworkin's use of 'interpretation' in his recent book *Law's Empire*[1] as a model for understanding the relationship between a judge and a body of law. As philosophy of mind seems to have supplanted philosophy of language as the engine of philosophical change so it may be that aesthetics in turn will provide a quarry for philosophy in the next decade much as it did in the early nineteenth century. Two signs of this are the importance that holism has come to have in recent years; organicism in the arts, a doctrine which has never gone out of fashion and indeed is evident in the very first writings on the arts, Aristotle's *Poetics*,[2] is obviously first cousin to global holism. (Although I say that it has not gone out of fashion it is curiously at odds with that post-structuralist form of hermeneutics which requires us to display, not the organic unity of texts, but their incoherence and contradictory nature. This is not an approach to the arts I share; indeed it is one which can be shown to be self defeating by arguments patent to most first year students of philosophy.) Indeed I think that the strong aesthetic appeal of philosophy may very well have to do with the way our concepts hang together so as to display an organic unity. Concepts have liaisons, it used to be said, and the tracing of the way one concept connects with others is part of the fascination of philosophy. The seamless web of our concepts ensures that problems illuminated in one area may reflect light on others. The second and more telling sign is the great interest in the concept of interpretation and in hermeneutics generally. To examine the philosophy of mind with the aid of concepts and ideas drawn from aesthetics may, then, be to anticipate developments elsewhere in philosophy. We shall, no doubt, see.

This conception of enquiry into the humanities and the social sciences contrasts sharply with a model which I shall describe as the 'hidden mechanism', 'systemic' or 'real essence model'. Before describing the hermeneutic model we therefore need a description of the alternative and it is to this that I now turn. But before I do so, there is one other prevailing theme whose presence needs to be advertised. It is the possibility of a non-realist theory of mind which contains within it a sort of surrogate or ersatz realism. This is an attempt to produce an alternative to essentialism which will none the less give us a determination of the truth or falsity of our judgments but without recourse to assumptions about levels of mental functioning.

II   SYSTEMS, MECHANISMS AND ESSENCES

Locke's distinction between real and nominal essence is a distinction which pertains to substances and not to individuals. Locke identifies essence as properties which no object can lack whilst remaining a sample of that particular natural kind. In Locke's famous words:

> it relates to sorts. The nominal essence of gold is that complex idea the word 'gold' stands for, let it be, for instance, a body yellow, of a certain weight, malleable, fusible and fixed. But the real essence is the constitution of the insensible parts of that body, on which those qualities and all the other properties of gold depend.[3]

Locke's conception of a real essence is of an underlying core which can explain the surface qualities of the material. Thus whereas the nominal essence of gold is that conglomeration of qualities which serve as our criterion for gold and in virtue of which we recognise a sample of gold as being gold, the real essence is the underlying molecular composition, the insensible parts on which the observable and criterial properties depend. This doctrine has come to be regarded, rightly, I think, as one of Locke's most profound and illuminating insights. Its influence on recent philosophy has certainly been considerable. Not only the realism of Harre and Madden shows its influence but the claim by Putnam and Kripke[4] that a word like 'gold' refers not to all samples sharing the same observable qualities but rather to samples sharing the same microstructure is also Lockean. Putnam makes the point in terms of the celebrated twin earth argument. If a distant planet had seas, rivers and lakes filled with a liquid identical in appearance and behaviour with water, even if they also called it 'water' in their language, it would not be water as long as its microstructure was different from that of terrestrial water. This holds even if the scientists of neither planet had the experimental technique to establish this.

We can accept that as science progresses we come to rely increasingly on microstructure to establish sameness of material without accepting Putnam's more extravagant claims, for it is a familiar criticism that Putnam's argument takes no account of the fact that these considerations can be more intuitively accounted for by a partial change in meaning; it is moot whether Locke himself thought that such an internal constitution might be discovered as science develops so that, say, by the invention of microscopy, we might be able to observe the underlying structure in virtue of which the observed surface characteristics are as they are. Although one would imagine that contemporary developments in optical instruments would have suggested this to Locke, my reading of the *Essay* suggests that it is not his view.

J.L. Mackie[5] argues that Locke believed that the proper use of natural kind terms was to refer to substances which shared the same underlying structure; if this is so then Locke anticipates Putnam. It is also worth noticing, parenthetically, that real essences may not be singular in form. They may, in fact, be a cluster of characteristics. So real essences may be plural. The molecular constitution may involve a combination of features or a multiplicity of layers.

The central question in this book, then, is whether a parallel theory of real essence is required for the human sciences. One variation on the 'hidden mechanism' theory may be immediately set aside; no theorist has suggested, to my knowledge, as some have argued with respect to the natural sciences, that an infinite series of levels of structure underlies human behaviour so that each level can be explained by the occurrences at a still lower level. However, more modest proposals are frequently to be found, notably in Freud and, more recently, in one of the most sophisticated forms of this theory, David Pears's *Motivated Irrationality*.[6]

It is a nice point in the history of ideas as to whether the notion of an underlying structure employed by Freud developed from a Lockean model of scientific explanation or not. I am inclined to think that the success of hidden mechanism explanations in nineteenth century science, together with Freud's undoubted early commitment to a scientific paradigm, influenced the development of his model of the mind. Freud's theory is in essence homuncular; in it sub-agents determine the surface behaviour of the individual. But homuncular theory has other antecedents than Locke; C.S. Lewis, in *An Allegory of Love*, shows how Guillaume de Lorris in *Le Roman de la Rose*[7] distributes the different facets of the character of the heroine among various embodiments such as Pride, Jealousy and Reason, thereby supplanting the person of the heroine entirely; here the sub-agents are personified.

What is unquestionable is that the conjunction of this with the idea of transformation which Marx drew from Hegel and Feuerbach proved intellectually explosive. Freud combines the idea that the psychoanalyst unmasks with the understanding of this unmasking in terms of deep structure. Just as Feuerbach stood the traditional relationship of God and man on its head, proposing that man creates God in his image, so Freud stood the traditional picture of passion and reason on its head. Instead of reason controlling passion, passion typically manipulates and cajoles the person into action, leaving the reason to rationalise. Beneath the surface of human behaviour are the warring agencies to which Freud gave the names of ego, superego and id; their conflict jointly determines our behaviour. There is an analogy with the way that, say, the movements of dust particles on a liquid, the Brownian motion, is thought to be determined by the behaviour of molecules beneath the level of observation, or with the germ theory of disease in which gross symptoms are explained by the invasion of the body by micro-organisms.

The Marxist account of the nature of capitalist society is another example of the hidden mechanism model transposed. On the surface of capitalist society we have various phenomena which seem to be systematically connected in a perfectly intelligible way, phenomena such as wages, prices, rents, profits, etc. but the real relationships between these are different. There is a gulf between how things appear to us and how they really are. Now the difference between this and the model case in the natural sciences lies in the fact that a failure to see the real relation shows not a lack of information so much as a blinding by preconception or prejudice. Significantly for the later discussions of this book, ideology is what conceals the real nature of the economic and social processes from us. This ideology is not merely a matter of self deception in one form or another; it is itself caused by the material basis of the economy. It is caused much as other superstructural features of society, the art, law, politics and the general culture of the society, are created by the economic base.

The important point is that Marx saw his task in terms drawn directly from the essentialist model of scientific enquiry; like the psychoanalyst the Marxist can break the surface and reveal the depths in terms of which the surface is rendered intelligible. 'Phenomenal forms are called "semblances", "appearances", "estranged outward appearances", "illusions", "forms" and "forms of manifestations".' The reality is described in terms which are surprisingly Lockean: 'essences', 'real nature', 'actual relations', 'secret or hidden substratums', 'content' and 'inner connections'.[8] The survival of class society depends on this distinction between appearance and reality because it is the way class society is presented to the proletariat which makes it believe, erroneously, that its interests are served by the status quo; it looks as though capitalism is in the interests of the labouring class even though it is not. Under socialism this gap between appearance and reality is said to vanish. Then the real nature of the relationships between people and production will not be disguised. Marx thinks of science as replacing an account of appearance by an account of reality in which the appearances are discredited. The sun appears to rise but science shows us that reality is different.

Perhaps it is significant that Marx in his early work and Freud in his later deserted scientific paradigms to some extent, though the matter is controversial. Marx's early writings express a moralist's denunciation of contemporary industrial society. Freud's later writings, particularly the *Introductory Lectures on Psychoanalysis* and the case studies, use concepts like 'meaning' and 'significance' which are difficult to square with mechanism although, on the other hand, the very late *Outline* shows as explicit a commitment to the hidden mechanism model as anything he wrote.

Cognitive psychology harbours more essentialists. Fodor's

9

doctrine[9] that beliefs are to be understood in terms of propositional attitudes towards formulae in an internal language, formulae which are token-identical with neurological states, does assume a distinction between two levels of mental functioning, one of which takes place in an internal language and which may be expressed to others in the external natural language with which we are all familiar. The very use of the metaphor of 'internal' betrays the theory which I wish to attack. Unless Fodor believes that mental functions only take place in an internal language and that their 'externalisation', to borrow a term from Collingwood's aesthetics, is not a matter of the mind at all, he is committed to a multi-level view of the mind. Whether Dennett[10] is a proper target of my strictures I am less sure. It does seem that the enlargement of intensional talk to computers and to parts of the brain is an application of these concepts to the physical parts of systems and not to sub-states of the mind. Indeed, on occasion, he seems to eschew a multi-level intensional account of the mind. But in his most celebrated doctrine, the idea that psychological explanation requires homunculi but that circularity or regress is avoided by assigning tasks to progressively more stupid homunculi until the process is discharged at a level when the homunculi are too stupid to be able to say more than 'yes' or 'no', Dennett seems close to the position under attack. This is, after all, classical homuncular theory.

There are in fact two possible positions here; one sees the hidden mechanism as consisting in features of the person which, in association with other, possibly environmental factors, lead to the observable behaviour. The other is a conflict model of the type advocated by Freud in which the interests of the sub-elements or sub-agents may conflict and where the consequent struggle creates the surface behaviour. Because the hidden mechanism or essentialist form of explanation is usually thought to be required to explain self deception and akrasia, both of which are cases of conflict, it is the second model which is most common. Thus the most recent advocates of a sub-system view of the person, David Pears and Donald Davidson,[11] adopt this view because they wish to explain irrational behaviour like weakness of will and self deception. Perhaps self deception more strongly suggests the sub-system model than does akrasia. In order to handle this without recourse to a sub-agent theory, I shall argue that self deception involves a species of weakness of will and that weakness of will does not require the sub-agent theory.

III THE ROLE OF NARRATIVE AND PARATACTIC

The task of this monograph is to give an account of interpretation and of what is sometimes called deep interpretation which does not use hidden mechanism explanations. Hidden mechanism explanations, I shall argue, are otiose in the study of man and his creations; they are hard to justify and are philosophically unwelcome. It is the conflict model which, as I have just implied, is my prime target. The role of interpretation is often to decipher, to unmask and to reveal what is hidden but this does not require an ontology of homunculi or sub-agents. Human behaviour, I suggest, can be explained in terms of narrative. The idea of 'depth' or of 'the hidden' needs reinterpreting in terms which are philosophically more defensible. The geometry of understanding persons is one dimensional.

The first task is to argue the case for our knowledge of persons. We can then adapt these arguments so as to make parallel cases for our understanding of society and of man's creations. What then are the arguments for rejecting a microagency approach to the mind?

First, the position under attack implies, though it is not identical with, the idea that the mind has parts. Now under what conditions do we pick out the parts of a whole? Imagine picking out part of the surface of a painting; this assumes that the part either already has boundaries or that the boundaries can be literally drawn on the surface or drawn in imagination. But it is more usual to pick out part of an object where there is a joint which separates it from the rest. We do this when we need to manipulate an object or to replace it in some way or another or to explain the way the whole functions. So there is often a technical or teleological aspect to the distinguishing of a part. The parts of a car can be disassembled and replaced. Equally the parts of the body can be functionally distinct.

Now the thinkers I criticise in this book distinguish parts of the mind. One factor, I have suggested, which prevents the individuation of parts from sinking into arbitrariness is the possibility of technical control. So it follows that one rationale for distinguishing parts of the mind would be of this form; thus if a cognitive psychologist separates memory and perception the assumption will be that this form of individuation is required to explain the function or to establish technical control.

The other case where we distinguish parts of a whole is where we separate, for example, the parts of a theory. This is not arbitrary because here the parts relate to a path towards the understanding of the matter. Axioms lead to theories or laws lead to predictions and this is the way to understanding. In this case the parts are our constructs. There is no question to be asked as to whether this coincides with a distinction in re.

So, assuming the classification is exhaustive, how do we understand the distinctions within a person proposed by essentialists? Either they are arbitrary or they reflect a mechanism or they distinguish parts as the parts of a theory are parts. The first and third are hardly possibilities which they would welcome. If the distinctions are arbitrary they are not worth the advocacy. And as regards the third they surely must think of them as parts in re and not merely as the consequence of an ordering of elements for pedagogic purposes. But there are problems in regarding them as parts of a mechanism.

1   First there is no obvious criterion for individuating the elements. They cannot be counted nor is there any clear way of distinguishing one from another. Freud distinguishes three sub-agents, ego, superego and id but, as Roy Shafer remarks, why stop at three? Some analysts add 'identity' as a fourth.[12] We might indeed individuate in terms of desires, reasons, beliefs, and motives. Each of these differs from the other and there seems no reason why we should not group together desires as one agent, reasons as another and so on. Alternatively we might choose to discriminate desires for the welfare of our children from desires for the welfare of others.

2   The first objection leads directly to the second. What criteria for distinguishing the agencies that are available are not topographical but grammatical. We individuate desires in terms of their intentional objects. One way of putting this is to say that, as a rule, desires have a nature which is disclosed in our knowledge of them. There are, of course, exceptions. It may be that an adolescent does not recognise his or her desires as sexual (and it may not only be true of an adolescent). But my desire for coffee is transparent. To know that I have that desire is to know what it is a desire for since a desire is a desire to do something in particular; its content marks it out. I shall expatiate upon this in chapter three. For the moment reflect on the distinction between a sub-agent and a group of desires and beliefs. At what point does such a group become an agent and at what point does an agent become a person? I have no idea of the answer but I do believe that defenders of sub-agency owe us an answer.

3   Enquiries take various forms. We can, in some cases, literarily

take the top off what we are examining. For example to take the cylinder head off an engine is to make the workings visible. We can imagine doing that with the heart, lungs or kidneys of a creature. The hidden mechanism model makes it seem as though some such approach is proper for persons. In fact our access to persons is not by penetrating the surface. Given a general presumption in favour of relating our ontology to our methods of enquiry we might be inclined to think that the hidden mechanism model is quite singular in its inappropriateness.

We require, however, some general grounds for thinking that the method we choose to use to investigate a given object reveals something about its nature or about its relationship to us. Such an argument has about it a transcendental cast, as indeed does each specific attempt to draw conclusions about an object from the method of enquiry we use. If the general and schematic thesis is true, that we can form true conclusions about the nature of the object of study from the method we use to study it, then the Popperian idea that the method of obtaining hypotheses is of merely psychological interest and that the scientific method is all to do with testing is certainly misleading. For this present argument should persuade us that we learn some very general facts about the nature of the typical objects of the domain of enquiry simply by noting the methods we use. Idealists will certainly be interested in this form of argument since they will question whether our understanding can outstrip the methods we use to acquire it. With this goes a belief that concepts are our creations and that we cannot expect more from them than has, so to speak, been designed into them. This assumption is deeply embedded in the approach I have taken here. Unless a concept has been so defined as to make its application dependent upon physical criteria which may, as yet, be outside the experience of ourselves and our experts, there can be no grounds for supposing that concepts have sharp boundaries and that radically unfamiliar cases can easily be placed within or outside their domain. We must beware of taking as paradigms the cases studied by Putnam and Kripke where concepts are designed so as to ensure that their application depends upon physical features which we may learn in the course of experience. The extension of this argument to the idea of sub-agents in the person yields a way of refining our second objection for it follows that there may be no non-arbitrary way of allocating desires and beliefs to sub-agents within the person.

Such an extension of concepts of beliefs and agency outside their normal purview can only imply that their application is a question of decision. Both Davidson and Pears conduct their debate at such a level of generality that the precise way in which the components are distributed is never discussed. But the beliefs cannot be distributed on grounds of consistency alone. For if people can be inconsistent then why cannot sub-persons be inconsistent as well. Freud certainly thought this; he explicitly casts the id as an agent for whom consistency has no claim.

In fact we shall not learn very much that is interesting about the ontological character of objects from the way we acquire knowledge of them in the great majority of cases. The bulk of cases are dull. Two cases in particular interest me and the contrast between them occupies the major part of this book. On the one hand are cases where we literarily look inside an object to see how it works. We may take the cover off an electric motor, open the chest cavity or investigate the activities of white blood corpuscles under a microscope. On the other hand, as I shall argue, we may analyse a literary or musical work by studying salient passages and drawing thematic conclusions about the significance of the work as a whole.

If an object does not possess the appropriate multi-layered structure, then we shall not discover anything by using the methods suitable for examining hidden mechanisms. It is a necessary truth that if we penetrate the surface of an object in order to see how its internal workings function, then it must possess that structure. The converse does not hold; it does not follow that if we are enquiring into an object which is complex in this way, we must therefore use these techniques. We might, through the deficiencies of technology or because we have reached the horizon of possible experimental technique, be forced to use other methods. We cannot use the method of dissection to investigate the nature of sub-atomic phenomena. We would, of course, then need other reasons for supposing the object is structured in the way it is and, with sub-atomic research, we have such reasons.

The theme of this book is that we have not understood the method by which we learn about the characteristics of human beings and that philosophers and psychologists have, too frequently, interpreted enquiry into the human mind on the hidden mechanism model. Admittedly, I have argued that we cannot assume that, because the techniques of investigation are paratactic and narrative and belong to the family of the arts rather than the sciences, that there is no internal mechanism of the sort postulated by Freud and others such as Eissler and Hartmann. For we have seen that statistical techniques may be used in the investigation of areas where we are confident there is an underlying structure. Equally it may be contingently advantageous to use techniques of thematic analysis in understanding persons even though the real nature of the person is multi-layered. But it does suggest that we need other strong arguments for believing in such a structure and I do not think those arguments are forthcoming. I shall argue that the problematic cases of self deception and akrasia can be understood perfectly well without such assumptions.

4   Finally, there is, perhaps, a tougher conclusion to be drawn. It is that there is no decent basis for dissociating explanation from the methods of enquiry in the way that thinkers from Freud to Fodor have. If we enquire into human behaviour via the thematic method, then that is how we explain human behaviour, so what explanation do we give when we postulate internal agencies such as homunculi? Fodor writes: 'We refine a psychological theory by replacing global little men by less global little men, each of whom has fewer unanalysed behaviours to perform than his predecessor.'[13]

Fodor is much exercised by the spectre of circularity but thinks he can avoid it. This is not the problem which alarms me. The suspicion of explanation *obscurum per obscurius* lies in the distance from ordinary explanation of human behaviour. I am not, incidentally, advocating any sort of conceptual conservatism. I am simply urging that reforming explanations should be sufficiently close to explanation as currently practised for there to be a recognisable continuity. Without such continuity they cannot count as explanation of beliefs, desires, character and personality. Thus Fodor says elsewhere: 'Understanding the operations of a computer capable of simulating a given form of behaviour is tantamount to understanding that behaviour itself.'[14] I cannot sufficiently relate this to our ordinary common sense understanding of a person for it to count as explaining his or her behaviour.

Kenny[15] has a parallel argument. The sub-agents cannot be said to know anything because the difference between knowledge and the storage of information lies in the relation of knowing to behaviour. Because sub-agents do not exhibit any of the behaviour which is criterial for knowing, they cannot be said to know nor can they be agents in self deception or inference or anything else.

Perhaps there are moral reasons for preferring a hermeneutic approach, with its emphasis upon the many different ways in which art, society and human behaviour can be understood. The multiplicity of interpretations of the behaviour of a person make possible a variety of lives and standards. Were we all judged by a single measure most of us would suffer by comparison with the outstanding.

Before I sketch the hermeneutic methodology which I propose as an alternative I need to say something about the form of causality to be found in action and how it differs from causality between material bodies. This occupies the next section.

IV CAUSALITY

In standard cases of causality, such as where a brick causes a window to shatter, the difference between where the impacting of the brick merely precedes the shattering of the window and the former causes the latter lies in the way that the nature of the first event brings about the second. There is something about the power of the brick to change the world. It is part of the nature of the brick and it lies in its internal constitution, what Locke called its 'real essence'. It is because it has the constitution it has that it has the effects it has. Harre and Madden,[16] in the standard account of the realist theory, called them 'powerful particulars'. But there are other recent presentations of the idea, lucidly by Galen Strawson. Strawson speaks of the causal powers of objects being possessed 'in virtue of the nature of the forces informing (and so governing) the matter of which they are constituted'.[17] Now, as elsewhere in this book, I am not attempting a metaphysical justification of this idea. It is sufficient that the idea is embedded in the conception of scientists. Scientists think that the universe is this way. The development of atomic and sub-atomic physics surely goes some way towards justifying that conception. Philosophical sceptics might, indeed, not countenance that these particles exist in re and so attempt the defence of a phenomenalist or instrumentalist interpretation of the facts, but I do not argue against that here. Even on such a philosophical reinterpretation, it is enough that there is a conception of science which is the target for a reductionist programme and about that there should not be a dispute. Of course, for much of the history of humankind, men have spoken of causal relations without having any such atomic picture in mind. But current conceptions of the relationship among both scientists and educated laymen involve this idea and this is all that is relevant to my discussion.

The view under consideration, then, is that in order to distinguish between regularity and causation we need the existence of objective forces in the things themselves. At a lower level, the smashing of the window is explained by the molecular changes brought about by the impacting of the brick. I do not know the precise story but I do know that there is one to be told. Such changes are contingently identical with the breaking of the glass. What happens when the glass is broken can be described in the language of microphysics. In much the same way a flash of lightning is contingently identical with a discharge of charged particles. The two identical events occur at the same place and at the same time and this is what entails the conclusion that they are in actuality the same. Equally, of course, this must be supplemented by a molecular story to be told about the brick.

Now if we take the view both that human actions are caused by our desires and that the model of causation is the standard one, it follows that we can only explain how the causality operates (and we need an explanation to distinguish it from mere succession) if an underlying mechanism exists which accounts for the way one causes the other. So the question which I set myself is how we can distinguish between a belief, desire, motive or what have you which causes my action and one which merely precedes it.

The way we have distinguished causality from succession depends upon the idea that the mechanism which underlies causality explains the difference. What will be required, then, to distinguish between succession and causation in the sphere of human action is the existence of a lower level of sub-elements whose mechanism brings about the effect. So if a desire causes an action, as many maintain, then it is necessary, if we are to find an analogy with the paradigm case of causality, that sub-elements of the desire bring about sub-elements of the effect. It is in the nature of the desire that its building blocks bring about changes with which the action is extensionally equivalent. Since the thrust of this book is against such a doctrine, it will not be surprising that I am sceptical.

First, desires seem integral. It is hard to imagine what elements or pieces of a desire could be like. No philosopher has offered the required sub-theory. Indeed, it is perhaps more obscure than the problem of distinguishing the parts of a person, the problem discussed in the last section; for now we are required to perform an even finer dissection, a dissection of desires themselves. In the case of actions pretty much the same applies. Of course, we could do a Tractarian reduction of the propositional form of a desire to its elements just as we could do a Goldman type of fine grained analysis of action. But the fine discrimination of parts in an action is not going to help. First, the Tractarian reduction of a desire to, say, an attitude and an object does not explain why the action follows. To be told what the desire and object are instead of having the more unspecific 'he wanted to' does not bring the necessity any closer and the strength of the 'hidden mechanism' accounts is exactly that they reveal to us the necessity lodged *in rerum*. So there is nothing here like the way in which a physical picture of the impact of a brick in unhooking molecules works. For there we have something like the mechanical model which some scientists thought necessary to physical understanding.

I suppose that another likely case of a sub-process at work is enthymenatic inference. I draw a certain conclusion from premises. The validity of this process is given by a sequence of operations which constitutes a proof. Now I may not go through all the stages and when I do not we have an enthymene. One sub-process theory would have me go through all the elements in my mind, subconsciously. But is there any reason to think this true? After all it was centuries before the valid forms were known and during this period human beings drew valid inferences; we know further that inferences can be formalised in different ways, so which of the sub-processes are supposed to exist in re?

Philosophers who insist that desires cause actions have two alternatives. Either they provide us with the theory they owe us or they admit the ambiguity of 'cause'. In 'Action, reason and cause', Davidson[18] remarked that we need the concept of 'cause' to distinguish those reasons which are available to me and that one or those on which I act. Only the latter cause my action. My problem here is to see whether a distinction can be drawn. Certainly in the case of the physical world we have a clear distinction between those events which preceded an effect and those which actually caused it . What I am asking is whether we can distinguish between those mental events which preceded an action and those which actually caused it. (To be more precise I should take the desire, belief or motive to be a state, the action to be an event and the 'triggering event' to be the recognition of an opportunity to act.) The answer I shall propose is that on the whole

18

we cannot, though there are grounds for making the distinction in some cases. Of course it might be arguable that there is a difference, though we cannot in general tell which of our reasons governs our action. I argue a stronger case in this book; we have no reason to think that, in re, the agent acted on one rather than another reason. Of course there are occasions on which we can say that, though a reason occurs to a man, his character is such that he would not have acted upon it. But this is merely to say that it will not be a reason for him. If I recognise x, y and z as reasons for doing a, then there is no reason to pick out one of these as the reason on which I act, nor even grounds for thinking that one of these reasons must be the producing cause.

I incline to the conclusion that there is no general distinction to be drawn between succession and causality in the sphere of human mind and action. If a desire, a reason, an intention or a motive precedes an action then it follows that the desire, reason, intention or motive causes that action, singly or in combination (or alternatively that there is succession but not causality). But there are some reservations to take into account.

But before I consider the caveats there seems one plausible account of the underlying mechanism which I have ignored. It is that the mechanism is to be found in the neural structure of the brain. Of all the neural events which are going on in my brain at any one time, one is identical with the reason on which I act and that neural event causes the bodily movements which are identical with the action. The problem is that Davidson, who must be a principal target here, does not, as far as I know, commit himself to such an account of causality. He seems to think of the causality of actions as autonomous and not necessarily reducible to the causality of brain and movement (though other philosophers certainly would endorse such an account). Its causal status certainly does not depend upon the availability of such a reduction. But there is a more general objection. This account requires investment into a very precarious industry, the identity theory, and its vulnerability can be given particular point by seeing how it presents problems in this context. The point about the physical model is that a more minute examination of the phenomena with the aid of instruments will reveal the structure in virtue of which the causality operates. But a more minute examination of a reason might show, perhaps, some hasty assessment of the situation, or some other degree of misdescription, but it will not show a brain event. Indeed the problem is, of course, that the enterprise is question-begging. We need to presume the identity of mental and brain events in order to provide a location for the mental events. For without such a theory we have no means of giving them that precise location which would enable us to establish an identity. Hence the evidence only warrants a causal tie or correlation between mind and brain, not an identity.

It is said by the materialists who seem to pervade the philosophical scene that the argument from the non-location of mental events is a bad argument on the premise that it conflates the event of thinking and the abstract object, the thought. But the distinction helps not at all. I am happy to say that I first thought of the arguments of this section in Finland but I certainly would not say that the event of thinking took place in my left hemisphere. The argument that it is question-begging is, in any case, not touched by this inept reply.

May we allow, then, that there is no way in which we can distinguish a sub-structure in these cases? Earlier, I argued that there are no arguments which show that such a sub-structure exists nor any way in which we can understand such a conception. So the idea that the forms of causality could be the usual form of hidden mechanism will then be unjustified. But this does not mean that there is no basis at all for distinguishing cause and succession. We shall come to an argument in a minute.

I have already mentioned Davidson's argument that causality is required to distinguish those reasons available to me from those on which I act. The distinction is sometimes presented as a contrast between those reasons which justify and those which explain. Now, at least sometimes, grounds for acting have to be recognised by the agent as grounds in order for them to have any causal force at all. I suppose that an agent could see what a particular proposition means without connecting it in any way with his intended action. In such a case it would not be a reason for him; consequently it looks trivial to say that a reason has to be recognised as a reason. As far as desires are concerned, the situation is not identical. I can have a complex of desires on which I may not act and which may not be grounds for action. I discuss this at more length in the context of akrasia.

It is also to be remarked that motives and desires could work their causal magic without being recognised to be doing so. It is enough that jealousy is a motive without our further recognition that we have that motive or desire; it has, however, to be registered that a recognition that we have an opportunity to act is of great importance to the causal force of the desire or motive. Indeed, to see why reasons are so intimately connected with rationality we need to understand the importance of conscious assessment here.

V

Now for the counter argument. Suppose a man forms an intention to act on the basis of a certain reason. The temptation must be to take the intention as supplying the extra causal force which converts mere succession into causal connection. This would hold equally if I act upon a whim. I suddenly decide for no reason to turn right at an intersection whilst out for a walk. There is no reason why I should do this. I just do it. Now surely here the intention turns the whim into an action; it supplies the causal force. So there is an additional feature which converts succession into causality. It is the intention. What I have said here about 'whims' might seem to have no special significance. Wherever there is an action which is preceded by an intention, it will be said, the intention causes the action. But whims are of considerable interest, as we shall see.[19]

Consider akrasia, which is, with inference and self deception, one of those areas where a hidden mechanism explanation seems plausible here because we think of the agent's behaviour as being determined by the conflict between sub-agents. In the conflict between reason and desire, desire wins. Now if we take an intention's preceding an action as all that qualifies it to be the cause of that action, then we have no explanation of one form of akrasia. This is not the classic form of akrasia where the agent acts not from prudence but from a desire and where he does not think his action right. Rather I am thinking of the case where, having formed an intention, he simply fails to execute. This is what Pears called 'brazen' or 'last-ditch' akrasia (though he is doubtful whether it can occur).[20] The point about this sort of akrasia is, of course, that it is inexplicable if not unintelligible. On a whim, the agent simply does not do what he intends to do. Since people do, sometimes, act on whim we can hardly view it as unintelligible though, ex hypothesis, we have no explanation. It is not unintelligible because it is part of the fabric or form of our life. Whereas in standard cases of akrasia we have an explanation in terms of the competing desire, here we have none. Providing, of course, that there is no reason not to act on a whim, acting on a whim is not irrational. But if there are positive reasons not to act, then acting on the whim is irrational.

Now one natural way of expressing the thesis that action from a whim is, of necessity, inexplicable is to say that it is an action which has no cause. So if I express an intention which embodies a whim, to present the intention as the cause does violence to the logic of the situation. I would think it natural for a causal theorist to take intentions as, *inter alia*, causes of action though I should say that Davidson's position on this seems to have changed from earlier remarks that 'intention' is syncategorematic to a more outright causal account.[21] But it is worth stressing that even within an account which takes 'cause' to be equivocal between actions and physical events I argue that intentions are not causes of action in the way that desires are causes of action; even if we allow that desires cause action in some special way not reducible to physical causation, some actions have no causes. It may be argued that I can act from a whim without it being true that my act has no cause. I may place a bet on a whim and it may be true that my act is caused by my seeing the man next to me place a bet on the same horse. Here my action has an explanation but no justification. Nevertheless it remains true, I think, that some actions are done on whim and that no causal account is readily available. I follow a particular path across a field whilst strolling. I do so on whim. There might be a cause – my desire to avoid a herd of cows – but there does not have to be. The field may be devoid of cows, horses or cow dung. Nothing explains the path I take and nothing justifies it.

If the action is intentional, indeed may be preceded by a consciously formed intention, yet has no cause, then it follows that the intention cannot cause it. So it cannot in general be true that actions are caused by intentions. But if we take an intention not to be a cause, how should we view it? The alternative is to take the intention as part of the act rather than preceding it; this solves the problem because it is a principle that nothing causes itself. But are there any pressing reasons in favour of this which are independent?

At this point a little excursion into accounts of the identity of action is called for. The familiar puzzle is how many actions there are when Jones kills Smith by shooting him? Is there one? Or is his levelling the gun distinct from his pulling the trigger which is distinct again from his shooting Smith which is distinct from his killing him? On the one hand there is no doubt that multiple charges can be brought against a defendant in law in virtue of what looks superficially to be one action. On the other there is the apparently devastating objection that Jones does not need to do anything else once he has fired the gun. The literature is vast and I do not want to do anything more ambitious than to cut the Gordian knot.[22]

The model assumed by those philosophers who think there is just one action under different descriptions seems to be that of the unity of a physical object which possesses many features and hence can be described in many ways. The same account runs *pari passu* for events and leads to the familiar claim that causality is extensional, that is that a causal statement remains true however one replaces the description of the cause of the effect. Just as a table may have a number of properties – its shape, age, colour, design, etc. – any one of which may be used to describe it, so an action or an event may be described in any one of a number of different ways.

I want to suggest a different model for the identity of an action, one which uses the pattern of the identity of a human being. The basis for the analogy is that an action takes place over time and that earlier sections of the action are related to later, much as earlier parts of the life of a person are related to later. Thus my present action in writing this book can be divided up into a number of sub-actions – my writing notes, my copying these on to the word processor, my thinking about the argument and correcting it, etc. It might certainly be convenient to divide this up into separate actions but what equally makes it a single action is the fact that it is informed by a single purpose and persists over time. It is the common intention which matters here.

Our life is composed of actions and the longer the projects or life plans the more they become identical with long stretches of one's life. Reading for a degree, writing a book, building a house oneself, or decorating the kitchen can thus seem projects which are, for long periods, identical with life itself. It is not at all surprising that they should have some of the properties of the life of a person.

So now to return to the problem of the relation between the intention and the action. I have argued that intentions do not cause the action. There are two main reasons for saying this. First, whereas reasons explain and justify an action, an intention does not. Nothing helps by citing an intention. Furthermore, and crucially, what explains the action also explains the intention. They have the same justifying or explaining antecedent. The second reason is that there are actions which are certainly intentional, such as some actions done on whim or actions done where there can be no reason for trying one rather than another of two alternatives. These are actions for which it is perfectly intuitively correct to say there is no cause. But if they have no cause, then *a fortiori* the intention cannot be the cause. Yet we will say, quite properly, that the agent acts intentionally.

I am assuming in all this that giving causes explains. Here no explanation is possible and none is required. To say that an action was done on a whim is to put it into a particular class. One way of resisting the thrust of my argument would be to open a gap between the idea of *x* causing *y* and the idea of *x* explaining *y*. Then there would be no reason to think that because *x* causes *y* that, under that description, *x* explains *y*. A statement of causality could be necessary; as Davidson argues, the necessity is a matter of the way it is described. We can describe the causal relation in a way which makes it contingent or in a way which makes it necessary. So an intention could cause an action but citing it would not explain the action. Then the facts that whims have no explanation or that the explanation of an intention is the same as the explanation of the action would have no special force. Well perhaps there is something in this. Certainly we need to choose our vocabulary in explanation of events and here Davidson's argument applies. But whether there is such an option open to us in the case of the action is far more debatable. Here causality is always explanatory. The problem is that we do not seem to have multiple features of reasons or motives in virtue of which we can choose between different ways of individuating them. There are no other contingent features which we could use to individuate them.

Do we then need to make a sharp distinction between doing an act intentionally and doing an act from an intention where the intention exists prior to the action. There seem some grounds for saying that there is only an accidental difference between an act done on a pre-existing intention and an act done intentionally where no prior intention exists. The greater iniquity of a premeditated crime is that it is like an action which takes place over a period of time during which the action could be left off. Given that the intention has exactly the same reason as the action and thus has the same cause, if we follow Davidson *et al.* in taking a reason to be a cause then we have some grounds for identity. So the intention is not an extra element which is added to the situation once the force of the reasons has been recognised. Rather, it is like an early stage in the action. This fits in with the general characterisation of action as a process given here. The action runs from the intention to its successful denouement. Not to act on an intention is more like breaking off an action in the middle.

An interesting conclusion follows from this. Even if we treat human action as governed by causality, the reign of causality is not universal. There are actions which are uncaused for we have no reasons for them. In this way it is utterly unlike the presumption of the universality of causality which dominates science and where exceptions such as in sub-atomic physics are a scandal. It is to concede areas of indeterminacy in the realm of the person.

My initial concern was, of course, with the objection that the difference between succession and causation in the mental lay in the existence of 'intentions' which provide the extra element required to turn succession into causality. I have rejected that by showing that intentions are not causes. There remains one final argument which I have yet to consider and which might offer some relief to the beleaguered Davidsonian.

We do have desires which are not acted upon. There are some which are experienced prior to action but which have nothing to do with it. In such cases there is a clear difference between causality and succession. In these cases it is the intentionality of the desire or indeed the reason which establishes what a desire or reason is for. It is my desire to drink a cup of coffee which makes it issue in that action and not another.

However, let us be clear as to just how limited a concession this is. It does nothing for the general Davidsonian problem as to how to distinguish between those reasons which are available to me and that one or more on which I act. For in this context we are concerned with the case where I may have several different desires, reasons or motives for performing one and the same action.

So, to conclude, the overall picture is something like this. The causality involved when an action is caused by a desire or a reason is distinct from the causality involved in physical processes. Unlike physical explanation, we cannot account for the difference between causality and succession in terms of an underlying mechanism. Indeed, in general we do not have a distinction between causality and succession in this area. The only qualification to this thesis is that the intensionality of the mental phenomenon is what selects one or more desire(s) as the desire for that particular action or thing.

VI

If, then, we reject a mechanistic conception of understanding persons what do we put in its place? The thesis of this book is that there are close similarities between our understanding of the arts and our understanding of persons and societies. In most fiction, drama or cinema, the characters are not constantly on stage and our impressions of them are as fitful as our impressions of our neighbours and our fellows. We interpret the behaviour of fictional and real characters on a par, eliciting more general dispositions and personality characteristics from the fragmentary encounters which provide us with a base. Furthermore, in the case of the work of art the entire work has a character given to it by the interpreter, a character which may or may not coincide with the character the creator intended it to have. The estimate of general character and disposition, both in art and in life, comes from educing thematic character from episodes which are themselves discrete and which suggest, rather than imply, the generalities. If I think of my neighbour as intolerant, I base this estimate on how he reacts in certain specified situations. He is not intolerant all the time. Often intolerance or tolerance are irrelevant to the situation in which he finds himself. It is inappropriate because the occasion is not one in which it is even possible to behave with intolerance. It is a disposition which surfaces from time to time like a stream which, flowing underground for most of its life, occasionally surfaces.

It is natural that the interpretation of a fiction mimics the interpretation of human behaviour. Hence it can come as a shock to find this deliberately disrupted by the writer. In Muriel Spark's novel *Loitering with Intent* the principal character acts as narrator, retailing the workings of an autobiography club whose members present notes on their lives to the narrator who, with the founder of the club, works these notes into coherent biographies. When liberties are taken with the notes it is as unclear to the reader as it is to the characters whether the results match what happened in the world or whether they are fantasy. The characters within the fiction have their own pasts revealed to them by a narrator placed within the fictional world.

Loitering with Intent here playfully recapitulates within fiction the relationship which holds in reality between understanding fiction and understanding real people. Both, after all, require the selection of certain episodes, images, metaphors, etc. as important, and the discursive elaboration upon these episodes in terms of a general theme. The general emerges in the particular. It is not observable aside from the individual exemplars. Nor need the author provide us with a key to the interpretation. Fiction is not usually allegory or *roman à clef*. But a first element in interpretation of whatever form is the selective foregrounding of passages which strike the reader, listener or onlooker as significant; this selective emphasis varies from individual to individual. The ideal situation is where a work of art has episodes or moments which catch our attention. They surprise, intrigue or delight us. Diaghilev used to say to his entourage 'Astonish me!' Now the passages which affect or afflict us are those which we, in the best cases, take as salient in our considered interpretations of the work. We think of *Macbeth* as about power and decision because these features display themselves in the soliloquies. When the passages which fascinate or even terrify prove to be those which emerge as salient in a thematic interpretation, the affective and intellectual aspects coincide with ideal effect. There is a further analogy to be found in the arts. The forms of thematic development which we find *par excellence* in the music of the first Viennese school also mirror the thematic understanding of the individual. Perhaps the understanding of fiction is at one remove from life; obviously we learn from fiction. But music offers the same processes of understanding at a second remove and at a greater level of abstraction than literature, film or drama. Take, for instance, religious and ideological commitments. These are not perpetually on view in the personality any more than other traits which we think of as characterising ourselves. They appear and reapppear on those occasions on which we 'act in character'. It is then that the character displays itself. The religious or ideological beliefs which give substance to their lives may be articulated in speech or action only at certain times. In bereavement, loss and danger we may think of people as revealing that true character. These traits are not a Humean thread which confers identity on the individual. Rather they are like 'deep' beliefs: though latent they show the stuff of which people are made. We shall see later that a man's deep beliefs often show themselves in what he is defensive about.

Of course, it may be said that the common round and daily task display the 'real' character rather than times of stress. Then it would be the reactive rather than the considered response which is more telling. Reactions could be at odds with our principles; equally, principles may modify our reactions. If, for example, somebody maintained conventional racialism when quizzed but acted with humanity when helping a black victim in an accident then we would, with some relief, think of the person as 'really' decent. The claims I make about paratactic and hermeneutical understanding of the person equally well describe this way of coming to know the real person. Whichever means we use to come to know sombody, the interpretative model fits.

Music matches the form of our lives in a parallel way. Because it has no propositional meaning, it is not discursive. It is structure rather than semantics which links music and life. Music, after all, contains no statements or assertions. It has no assertion sign and its elements have no sense. However, when we are analysing the structure of a piece of music we proceed by the same means, the excision and display of salient elements. By this we show the general character of the work.

In these respects the characteristic form of thematic analysis is preserved.

The actions which compose my life, however, have a meaning in that they are intended and can be seen as the consequence of plans. So a narrative account rather than a chronology which merely recounts a sequence is what is normal for human action and agency; it is the form in terms of which the agent presents his behaviour to himself and in terms of which he customarily plans his life. So the relationship of an episode in an individual's life to his life as a whole is not like the relationship of an instance to a generalisation in science. It is not inductive. It is more like the interpretation of an episode in the narrative of a novel for here we can select so as to exhibit, say, a craving for affection or a need for security or a pervasive need to help others. There is no equivalent significance in music.

A hint in this direction is to be found in Milan Kundera's splendid novel *The Book of Laughter and Forgetting*:

> It is no wonder then that the variation form became the passion of the mature Beethoven who (like Tamina and like me) knew all too well that there is nothing more unbearable than losing a person we have loved – those sixteen measures and the inner universe of their infinite possibilities.
>
> This entire book is a novel in the form of variations. The individual parts follow each other like individual stretches of a journey leading towards a theme, a thought, a single situation, the sense of which fades into the distance.
>
> It is a novel about Tamina, and wherever Tamina is absent, it is a novel for Tamina. She is its main character and main audience, and all the other stories are variations on her story and come together in her life as in a mirror.[23]

Interestingly this has a parallel in recent psychoanalysis; Heinz Lichtenstein[24] describes an individual living out variations on an identity much as a musician might play out an infinity of variations on a single theme. The difference is that in life we discover the theme by abstracting it from its various forms. The burden of this book is that the structural parallels run from music and fiction to life itself and indeed that the understanding of persons who live their lives parallels the understanding of art in moving from parataxis to syntaxis. Let me explain.

The elements in the original text which literary interpreters or indeed psychoanalysts have to interpret are paratactic. The sayings or sections are listed without connection by syncategoremata. Take the quotations from any essay in literary criticism, place them side by side and you have the ingredients of an interpretation paratactically arranged. They do not make continuous sense until they are linked in interpretation. Interpretation is a process which leads from parataxis to syntaxis. Of course, the effect of such a paratactic arrangement may well be that the reader immediately jumps to a conclusion embodying a thematic overview before the discursive links arrive. But the next stage is normally the discursive presentation of these elements. Now this may well involve metalinguistic elements in as much as the quotations are embedded in a text. This holds for Freudian as well as literary interpretation; on the Freudian theory the arrangement of the material of the analysis is, in fact, paratactic. The original form is a connected narrative and the paratactic is created by taking elements out of context in quotation. For the analysand's recollection is typically fragmented and incoherent. Items are displaced and their interconnection obscure. It is a fractured narrative which lacks intelligibility. One central task of the analyst is to reconstruct the original narrative and re-present it to the patient in a form which he can understand and, through his acceptance of it, find adjustment.

So the Freudian case mimics both fiction and life. The primitive narrative, if one existed, is now lost. The patient presents the analyst with a story which makes little consecutive sense as it stands. It has both to be refashioned in such a way that the elements themselves are given a sense by showing what they symbolise and then also reassembled into a coherent unity. So what interpretation does is to produce a syntactic account which subsumes the discrete elements of what the agent thought, said or did. It is worth comparing this with Norman Holland's well-known theory;[25] he argues that our ways of coping show in all our behaviour and our reading of literature must be included in this. Thus our fantasies or defensive tactics will infect our methods of interpretation. The themes we discern mirror our own make-up.

To Holland there is, I think, an obvious rejoinder. Do we learn from fiction? Does it enlarge our sympathies? If the answer is in the affirmative then it cannot be that our understanding is merely a projection of our own character.

The task of the analyst is, then, the recovery through a process of paratactic rearrangement of a hypothesised syntactic original which the patient has distorted, displaced or repressed. It is as though a text has been largely lost and from the fragments which remain the analyst attempts to recreate the original. But the analogy is not exact. The original is a sequence of events now past, experiences which may or may not have been present as a totality to the consciousness at any one time in the past. There is no reason to suppose that the patient knew of all the causal interconnections at any one time. Imagine reading a novel over a long period during which most of the action is forgotten by the reader, or recalled only in a significantly distorted form.

If, as I have suggested, music imitates the form taken by interpretation in the literary arts, what do we say about interpretation in music? In both cases we have a text. A form of functional analysis like that of Hans Keller gives us a paratactic reorganisation of the score which may itself be used in a linguistic discussion of the score using the elements which have been extracted as examples. Since the original quoted material is not propositional in form the interpretation is not metalinguistic as it is in the case of literary criticism. Ideally the interpretation as performed renders clear the ideas of the interpreter about the work. It does this by emphasising or foregrounding those parts of the work around which the interpreter's conception of the work centres. What makes this, in music, a purely formal matter is the lack of any semantic content in the foregrounded episodes. Music does not contain propositions. This elementary fact allows a largely structuralist picture of the nature of music and its interpretation. For, as we have seen, the elements in the paratactic organisation have no sense.

The sense in which an interpretation in performance, as opposed to an interpretation in the form of a writtten analysis, is paratactic is oblique. The conductor who presents his interpretation of the work does so in the course of presenting the text, and in this he does not differ from the theatrical interpreter. The music is consequently given as text in performance at the same time as, by his own choice of tempi, accent, phrasing, etc., the interpreter presents his own view of the work. There is no dissection and the structure is unimpaired. If we turn our attention to the structure of the interpretation, that is to the way in which certain episodes are foregrounded, then the structure of our attention is paratactic. We pay attention in such a way that certain parts obtrude. Unlike the literary critic, the musical interpreter does not embed foregrounded episodes in a new syntactic structure. Even if he writes about the work, what he quotes is devoid of semantic significance. But at least in one very important respect music draws very close to life; for the way in which the interpreter, and we, grasp a particular view is by an implied paratactic rather than an actual one. We pay attention to certain aspects of the behaviour and character of a fellow human being. It is the role of selective attention which leads me to describe this as requiring the 'paratactic imagination'.

When the formal development of music became sufficiently advanced to permit the grand and intellectually satisfying structure of a Bach fugue or a Haydn sonata movement, then music, in Kundera's words, left 'the stage of idiocy'. I have argued that this structure can only be grasped by an analysis of the music which presents the themes and that such an analysis depends upon a paratactic organisation of the original. Adorno[26] pours scorn on what he regards as the fetishism of the culture industry whereby the listener can only pick out the famous tunes. Whatever the vulgarity of this procedure, the recognition of themes is a condition of the intelligibility of music, and the difficulty of contemporary music begins here, as everybody knows. Adorno admires Schoenberg's atonalism as a blow struck at bourgeois culture. I rather view it as the historically inevitable decline of music from a pinnacle where thematic integration and key structure gave it a unique stature. The arguments presented here show music to be not, as Adorno suggests, windowless monads which represent society through unselfconscious representations but structural representations of the life of the mind.

Whilst he was in a sanitarium, Barthes read all the works of Michelet, copying on to cards those sentences which he found amusing or striking. 'In arranging these cards, a bit as one might amuse oneself with a deck of playing cards, I couldn't avoid coming up with an account of themes.'[27] We could scarcely have a clearer account of the paratactic process. Barthes described these fragments as 'lexias'. However, the lesson he drew was very different from the one I have drawn. The intertextuality which Barthes precipitates is supposed to undermine the idea that in a work of art the detail contributes to the whole. Now since it is precisely by this method that we can see how detail and the whole connect, the conclusion is mystifying. For the point about art is that it is by our selective attention to detail that our judgement of the whole comes about. If music is jocular or high-spirited, or if a play is a study of reconciliation, the judgement is backed by quotation and quotation is by nature selective.

Abrupt modulations, unprepared dissonances in music or disconnected narratives in drama or literature or any sudden change of direction draw our attention to the possibility of a paratactic, and analogies can be found in the other arts. Adorno instances the use of montage in the cinema. Perhaps a more extended usage of these techniques is flashback. Nicholas Roeg's film *Bad Timing*, through flashback, presents a psychoanalyst's recollection of his own affair. The paratactic form of this mirrors the way the patient recounts his experiences to the analyst; the analyst's task of interpretation in which the film's audience is enagaged neatly mirrors the analyst's task with respect to his own past. The curiosity of the audience is aptly matched by the curiosity of the patient who wants to know everything about, and to possess completely, the woman with whom he is infatuated.

The fractured and disconnected narratives which are to be found in the classics of modernist literature such as Biely's *Petersburg* and Joyce's *Ulysses* are typical of modern art. The understanding of the person which they parallel is an understanding of those persons or those aspects of a person which are difficult to interpret, which are subtle and elusive. A striking recent illustration which exemplifies the divergence between nineteenth-century and contemporary conceptions of narrative is the remarkable dramatisation of *Bleak House* by Hopcraft and Devenish which imported a contemporary fragmented character to what was, whilst perhaps atypical, a product of the nineteenth century.

Looking at the arts generally, though, it is clear that the procedures which we require for the interpretation of classical music and literature are now often incorporated into the works themselves instead of requiring action by critic, listener or reader. Barthes remarks that there is a sense in which modern art is all surface and spectacle. If interpretation involves, as I think it does, identifying themes via a paratactic interpretation of the original, then the discontinuities of modern art so vividly described by Marshall Berman[28] place that paratactic on the surface. This might be the sense of Barthes's claim. However, this does not preclude a further paratactic in which elements are again withdrawn from the text and juxtaposed.

The type of interpretation in which we are mainly interested takes the narrative as its subject matter and it is for this reason that the approach I advocate presupposes a narrative conception of the mind. We describe both a fictional character and his world and the behaviour of others in the form of a story. However, a psychoanalytic study may not always take this form. An analysis may well contain quotations from what the patient said to the analyst and from this point on the similarity to critical interpretation may be more striking than the resemblance to a story; for interpretation, as I argue, involves paratactic rearrangement. In the same way, the forms of interpretation presented in the performing arts may well require the fragmentation of the performance in order to make the interpretative points clear.

If narrative is the first form of the interpretation of a person's behaviour (and it counts as interpretation simply because it cannot contain all the events of the life but must select), the second, the critical stage, involves the sectioning of this narrative and its reorganisation in imagination or fact; this is a precondition for the forming of thematic judgements about the character. The rearrangement makes possible those biographical judgements which vary in depth and interest from the average employer's reference to the work of a Boswell.

One important consequence of this approach is that the model of textuality, so widely canvassed in recent writing about psychoanalysis,[29] becomes less sustainable; for the model of the text assumes a synchronic understanding, whereas the understanding of a person or society requires the interpretation of an entity persisting through time; such a diachronic model requires thematic analysis. So, in important respects, the model of a text is very misleading as an analogy. The understanding of a text is not selective until we interpret. The simple reading of a text is not a good analogy for the understanding of a person whereas the interpretative understanding of a relatively large-scale text is.

I have stressed the analogies between understanding art and understanding persons and their creations. There are, of course, disanalogies. A work of art is a completed entity whereas persons continue to change through their lives. In some important ways film or drama are dependent upon our first being able to understand persons; of course, subsequently our understanding of persons may be influenced by our understanding of art. Indeed one of the important ways fiction deepens our understanding is by emphasising the indeterminacy of judgements about others in a way that ordinary life may not. We may not have occasion to notice the extent to which the complexity of others undermines the simplistic moral judgements we tend to make. Fiction can remind us. In later chapters I shall make much of this indeterminacy because it connects with the place interpretation has in understanding people.

2

HERMENEUTICS AND
ANTI-REALISM

The either–or encapsulates our inability to bear the essential
relativity of human affairs, an inability to come face to face
with the absence of a supreme arbiter. This inability means
that the novel's supreme wisdom (the wisdom of uncertainty)
is hard to accept or grasp.

(Milan Kundera)

I

In rejecting a hidden mechanism model for the understanding of
persons, their creations and their institutions, I have said little
about the positive features which mark out objects as suitable
subjects for hermeneutic enquiry; although not all I say is entirely
uncontroversial, I propose five marks which commonly register
differences in kind between the objects of hermeneutics and those
of natural science.

First, in the arts and human sciences we deal with human
actions and their consequences. This is not to say that what we
examine will always have been planned or foreseen by the agents
who bring them about. The independent actions of many agents go
to make up the market. Unforeseen and unintended consequences
make up the range of objects as much as the foreseen and intended.
It is a cliché that political action brings about consequences which
may be quite contrary to what was desired. The implications of
what Shakespeare put into the mouth of Hamlet are hardly likely
to have been fully worked out. Religion may have the function of
being an opiate of the people without any bishop, priest or deacon
intending that it be so.

Second, the objects which we interpret are singular; they do not fall into groups which have features in common but each has to be taken on its own merits and in context. We do generalise, of course, but when we do we use the original as a source of suggestions as to how we may treat the new case, suggestions which may prove helpful or unhelpful. It is more like a source of hypotheses than an inductive basis. Whereas if one pure sample of mercury displays certain physical characteristics we know that any other will, we cannot assume that because a certain practice has a significance in one society it will have the same meaning in a neighbouring society. It might or it might not, though it may make good sense to proceed on the assumption that it does, especially if the societies have a common history. But a practice which has one significance in one context may have quite another one in a different context. The same principle holds in the arts. Thus the quotation from Spenser in *The Waste Land*, 'Sweet Thames run softly till I end my song', cannot have the same effect as it does in the original. In Eliot it is parodic and slightly puzzling. Indeed the concept of meaning or significance, as many writers have observed, does not have any place in the physical sciences. If it is used there then it is an extended use. We typically explain the significance of a device, feature or practice by showing what the agent intended to achieve by using it.

Traditionally one mark of the hermeneutic has been the so-called 'hermeneutic circle', the doctrine that the understanding of the whole comes from the understanding of the parts and yet the understanding of the detail in turn determines the understanding of the whole. So we have a pre-understanding or fore-understanding of a text, a society or a work of art which we modify as we see the detail. We see that this is a statue of a rider and we see the hand as pulling on the rein. Yet, at the same time, the pulling displays a nervous tension which suggests the fear of the rider and thus changes our grasp of the whole.

Another feature which encapsulates the way in which my own personal background enters into the business of interpretation is what is fashionably described as 'foregrounding' (a term introduced by the Prague Structuralists), though 'salience' is as good a term as any. It is hard to see how interpretation can have the features it has if we are not free to select within the whole those features which are important. This is of obvious importance in the arts. If I am to defend a certain interpretation of Shakespeare's *Hamlet* then I do so by referring to certain passages and these will be passages which I foreground. Thus no intelligent reading of *Hamlet* will fail to take into account the soliloquies. From the fact that they are the natural starting point it does not follow that this foregrounding is forced upon us. But both practice and the conventions of dramatic understanding within which Shakespeare wrote take the soliloquies to be central. Certainly we could base an interpretation on other features of the play. But any interpretation which relegates the soliloquies to secondary status would be difficult to defend and seems eccentric. Presumably a defence would be that the play became richer and more intelligible thereby. But to show this we would have to relate the interpretation to a tradition of practice and understanding which has its roots in the culture from which the play derived. Certainly judgements of salience may vary from person to person. It is, after all, here that understanding most evidently depends on the idiosyncrasies of the individual. The role of critical tradition is to set bounds upon such variation.

A final feature raises much larger and philosophically more interesting issues and brings me to the centre of the discussion. This is what is described as the underdetermination of interpretation. On this view, interpretations go beyond the facts; they are quasi-speculative advances on the evidential basis. The point about interpretation is that it is not fully accounted for on the basis of what the text offers. Thus a pianist's interpretation of a Beethoven sonata must go beyond the notes; the notation is not specific; he must decide just how fast is *allegro con brio*, just how loud is *mf* and how to interpret the marking *con amore*. But underdetermination also connects with the matter of selection; in literature, to say that Christopher Marlowe's *Dr Faustus* is a play about knowledge, about the relation of knowledge of the world to self knowledge and about knowledge of means and knowledge of ends, as Cleanth Brooks does,[1] is implicitly to select some passages as of greater importance than others; some speeches are emphasised and the selective emphasis is internally related to the underdetermination of the interpretation. The text does not tell us what we have to emphasise. Certainly there may be inherited conventions of understanding in both literature and music which give us guidelines on interpretation but they do not rigidly prescribe. That they do not allows the existence of other viable interpretations. Even if the text excludes some, others remain compatible with it. Equally if I advocate a Marxist view of history it is on the implicit selection of economic forces as fundamental in a way that a historian who views political factors as basic might not allow, though there is evidently a larger story to be told here.

On the face of it this does not distinguish between interpretation in the humanities and explanation in the natural sciences. For a given set of data can always be explained in terms of competing physical hypotheses. The simplest non-trivial example is fitting a curve to a set of points on a graph. At school we were taught to fit the simplest curve. But there really is no overwhelming reason for doing so. An infinite number of curves would fit the same points. Scientific explanations are also underdetermined by the data. So can anything be done to revive the distinction between hermeneutic understanding and scientific explanation?

To do this, we need to look more deeply at what we presuppose about the two continents of human enquiry. I believe that we assume one to be realist in principle and the other non-realist. Before going further a caveat is required; of course, there have been positivists and instrumentalists in science, Mach and Eddington, for example. But not only is this untypical but, I believe, such a stance runs counter to the concepts we use in scientific investigation; as I remarked in the last chapter, my claim is essentially a conceptual one.

We need to distinguish two forms of realism. The first takes realism to be asserting that events, things or qualities have some sort of existence independent of our say-so. They are out there, so to speak, part of the furniture of the world. A realist about moral qualities, for instance, will claim that, as well as physical qualities such as rectangularity, density and opacity, there is a second group of qualities such as moral rightness or wrongness which attach to actions or to goodness or badness and which are properties of states of affairs. I shall call this 'ontological realism'. A useful figure which expresses this thought is that of there being a 'God's eye view' of the world.

The second form of realism is 'right answer realism'. There is no good nomenclature available so I shall call it 'surrogate realism', without much hope that the terminology will catch on. Indeed the word 'surrogate' always suggests the implication that ontological realism is a preferred metaphysics and in as much as I concede this implication I adhere to the scientific model. The idea is that realism lies in the existence of a right answer to questions we might raise about the objects of investigation. For example, one form of moral realism will assume that the answer to a moral dilemma exists in advance of any enquiries we might make; another and perhaps more plausible form is possible in which the right answer is, so to speak, created in the course of ethical deliberation. Take the case of a man who cannot make up his mind whether to leave his wife for his mistress. He goes through all the issues as honestly as he can, neither placing his own interests and well-being above those of the other two combatants nor dismissing them as irrelevant. Eventually he reaches a decision. We can easily allow that, at least in many cases, there will be no gap between his procedure and the answer. The rightness of the answer lies in the fact that he has gone through this procedure to reach it; there is no self deception and there are no logical blunders in the deliberative process. What more can we ask for? We can neither say there is an answer outside this particular deliberation nor can we say that any answer counts as the correct answer.

In science, ontological realism entails surrogate realism; the idea is that one puts to nature a question the answer to which exists independently of the enquiry; the answer is there, waiting to be found out. The point is that one could, of course, be a surrogate realist at least in some domains without being an ontological realist. Let me illustrate. The writer of a fiction describes, as we rather fancifully say, a possible world which is inexactly specified. It is not determinate. We do not know what Hamlet was doing whilst Horatio was first observing the ghost. But although this is so and although there is no question of ontological reality here because Hamlet does not exist and never did exist, nevertheless we can imagine that a procedure might be devised for answering questions which arise. When asked by a correspondent what Elizabeth Bennet's favourite colour was, Jane Austen replied. We can easily imagine an extension of this procedure by, say, a guild of saga writers, empowered to answer any questions readers might raise about the characters. Quite possibly this is already done with respect to a television or radio serial like *The Archers*. However, we might get, through this, unhappy inconsistencies which are irresoluble save by the fiat of an appeal court whereas there are no inconsistencies in re; the world always has the right answer. Be this as it may, a guild or an appeal court can give a right answer to enquiries, an answer which is neither determined in the course of deliberation nor predetermined by the fabric of the world. Here any consistent answer will do providing the right authorities offer it.

If the concepts in question refer to objects which exist independently then a well-formed question, for example, as to whether the AIDS virus has the postulated structure, has an answer before we set about our investigation. In this it is clearly different from the parallel question which might puzzle the jurisprudent, about whether there is a right answer as to whether a murderer should inherit as a result of his crime; such an answer can hardly be supposed to be determined by the way the world is irrespective of judicial precedent or law. The way the world is determines the answer to the question about the Aids virus. The judge may have to decide whether the murderer should inherit as a result of his crime. I have argued elsewhere that yet another case is the way in which a cure may be manufactured by a psychoanalyst who persuades the patient (or client) to adopt his narrative of the patient's earlier life. Once he sees it in the terms prescribed then the causal power of the trauma may be altered but it is altered by his accepting a redescription which is, of itself, neither true nor false.

It may also be worth distinguishing the cases in which I am interested from the cases where the concept is ill defined. Traditionally such cases are connected with the sorites paradox or with such chestnuts as 'baldness'; it may not be clear whether a man is bald or hirsute because the concept is not sufficiently well defined to provide an exact dividing line between baldness and non-baldness. This, of course, may be no deficiency in the concept; it depends upon what we want it to do, on what our interests are in the situation.

The arts are rather different again and provide further evidence, were evidence needed, that 'interpretation' is a 'family resemblance' concept. Suppose we assume that what makes a work of art great is the verdict of a consensus of critics. This is a view which is pretty widespread (though not quite right as stated, in my view). Then in a case where the consensus has not met a work has, on this theory, no determinate value. But nothing follows from this about the indeterminateness of the concept of artistic greatness. We should not conclude from the fact that the concept has not been applied in a particular case to an individual that the concept is ill defined.

Many cases can be distinguished. For example, one form of realism about mathematics takes there to be Platonic objects to which mathematical statements correspond if true. One form of anti-realism rejects this. A second form of realism takes there to exist answers to questions set about, say, the truth of Goldbach's conjecture, prior to enquiries. A second form of anti-realism denies this. The first form of realism is ontological and the second surrogate. A third case of surrogate realism occurs where an answer can be created but its creation is internal to the process of enquiry which leads to it. In none of these cases, be it noted, is there any question of the concepts concerned lacking definition.

Even this categorisation oversimplifies. For a non-Platonist who is also a realist, it may be that the answer to Goldbach's conjecture exists antecedently to enquiries, but it certainly will not exist independently of mathematical concepts. It is because there are these concepts, and concepts are, for a non-Platonist, the products of human activity, that we can have matters of issue like that of Goldbach's conjecture. But we could not have such a question if we had no procedures of enquiry at all. They have to exist as a general practice.

In hermeneutics we have a most extreme form of anti-realism. At least in some cases our enquiries, no matter how complete, will not produce an answer which can be said to be true or false. There is no correct answer to the question as to whether Marlowe's *Dr Faustus* is really about knowledge. It may be an interpretation which is enriching or impoverishing but it is not right or wrong. For where would the correct answer reside? Not with Marlowe, for great writers write better than they know and his absorption of his culture ensures that his words have connotations and significances of which he may, at best, be only half aware. Not with the text because the point of interpretation is that it goes beyond it. The point is still clearer in the performing arts. The Busch and Lindsay quartets may play late Beethoven differently but we would be reluctant to say that one is right and the other wrong. Of course there are interpretations we may rule out of court without much in the way of a second thought; we might say that to take a whole hour over the first movement of op. 135 cannot be right. Turning to another field of enquiry, when the American historian Hayden[2] claims that the Renaissance exhibits three distinct intellectual movements it seems strange to ask whether this really is the case and whether it does not, after all, contain two or four. The point about the claim is how it articulates and renders intelligible the period of history under examination.

Perhaps it is the very uniqueness of the objects under investigation that brings about these typical features. In the case of moral dilemmas of the sort I described, or of works of art, the individuality of the case ensures that there are no criteria which determine decisions in such hard and complex moral cases and no criteria which decide the evaluation of art. This being so it is inevitable that if a decision is to be reached, its rightness or wrongness will not depend upon its conforming with external standards. Thus the way is paved for the typical features of these cases, that it is in the process of arriving at the verdict that the rightness or wrongness lies.

What I am suggesting, then, is that in the physical sciences we conceive of our researches as discovering and not creating the objects which we investigate. Nature has a structure and obeys laws independently of us; our speculations either match or fail to match the way things are. The anti-realist aspect of humanistic enquiry displays itself in the way that interpretation floats free of the facts just where understanding of those facts is expressed in an intellectual creation which is circumscribed but not determined by those facts.

In the arts this is hardly news. Although there are dissenting voices, the consensus is that interpretations co-exist with their rivals and there is no procedure for discarding all but one of the competing accounts. In the social sciences, however, much of the history of theory and methodology has been the history of attempts to understand people in terms of the model of science and especially that model where we postulate a lower level of phenomena which creates the observable phenomena which we are trying to explain. A good exemplar of the model is the germ theory of disease, where the visible symptoms are caused by an underlying mechanism not visible to the naked eye: the invasion of the body by bacilli. The two sorts of realism go together here; if you believe that there is an underlying mechanism which determines the surface phenomena and which exists independently of it, then you will also believe that there is a pre-existing answer to questions which you raise about it. The gist of the hermeneutic approach I advocate is that there is no parallel in the case of the arts, no parallel in many areas of enquiry into the human mind and no parallel in many areas of enquiry into human products and human institutions. We may call this feature, that well-formed questions have no answer, indeterminacy. Indeterminacy, I argue, is displayed in a whole range of human enquiries. But we must start with the indeterminacy of the mental.

The indeterminacy of the mental is a fashionable doctrine and it can bear several constructions. The first, brought to our attention recently, is that no list of mental facts can be given. To list what I believe requires the inclusion of consequences of my beliefs such as negative existentials which may be infinite in number and are certainly indefinite in that I cannot at any time list their extent. Thus I believe that there is no replica of me living in the town of Llanelli but I also believe that I have no replica in any other portion of space. By the sub-division of space and time, the things which I believe easily become infinite in number. I did not, of course, consider any of these beliefs until I began writing this paragraph. These features of my mental life make a computer representation of the beliefs which I hold an impossibility because an indefinite or infinite number of mental states cannot be mapped on to a finite machine. Of course, we could always ascribe to a computer negative existential beliefs in the same way as we do to ourselves. But once this has been done the point of the analogy has been lost. We no longer use the computer as the basis for cashing beliefs into hardware but treat it on a par with persons.

The thesis of the indeterminacy of the mental is commonly associated with Donald Davidson.[3] Davidson argues that we cannot ascribe beliefs on a one-by-one basis; beliefs cohere with other beliefs, desires, preferences, hopes and intentions so that our ascription of beliefs is based upon a holistic or global apprehension of patterns in behaviour. So to form a theory about an individual may require a compromise between what one or more separate features suggest. Between two or more interpretations there may be no way of choosing. We interpret the whole pattern and this interpretation is underdetermined by the factual basis. Bruce Vermazen[4] construes Davidson as suggesting that there are no mental facts. But this could be either taken as indicating that the evidence does not favour one or other of two alternative interpretations, or it may be taken as suggesting that there is no hidden fact of the matter available to an omniscient observer. Davidson's view is the former. But in either case rather than claiming that a unique answer cannot be found, the Davidsonian view is that no unique answer exists at all.

The claim that there are no mental facts looks *prima facie* implausible. If it is taken to imply that there is no evidential base on which our interpretations are erected then this seems to allow nothing that could be the subject of interpretations. It is rather similar to the deconstructionalist claim that no text has a meaning independently of the interpretations which we make. But unless there is some common ground from which we start there is no means of comparing interpretations and this we quite certainly do. If the claim that there are no mental facts, on the other hand, is intended to suggest that mental talk is nothing but an interpretation of observable 'physical' behaviour then the thesis comes close to logical behaviourism, the doctrine that the basis for the ascription of 'mental terms' is behavioural and that nothing lies beyond the gross facts of behaviour. But I may believe that there is no separate and more fundamental group of facts about human beings to which 'mental terms' refer, a realm which both causes and explains behaviour and to which perhaps we each have private access, without my being a logical behaviourist. My anger is not reducible to my behaviour. My behaviour expresses my anger but no internal collection of facts is being expressed in this behaviour. There is nothing over and above it.

Dennett suggested a radical view of these 'mental facts'.[5] He considered in his Rylean early work that mental terms might not refer. To think that beliefs refer is perhaps as egregious as thinking that 'sakes' and 'behalfs' refer because we can use them in phrases like 'on behalf of' or 'for the sake of'. They are not things that can be mislaid, inspected or handed over to the police.

Writing in a different and a Wittgensteinian tradition, Lars Hertzberg[6] brings the discussion closer to the main topic. He argues that one lesson to be drawn from late Wittgenstein is that the indeterminacy of the mental in the attribution of motives and feelings brings a kinship with moral and aesthetic appraisals. 'The uncertainty is constitutional. It is not a shortcoming.' However, Hertzberg does not think we should conclude that judgements about the mental have no truth value. There is a transition between cases where there seems no doubt about the facts and where judgements can be agreed to be true or false to cases where it is clear that we are dealing with a matter of interpretation. Hertzberg is surely right about this. Cases of self deception or akrasia are often cases where more than one opinion may be plausible. Contrast that with the ascription to me of the knowledge that there is a word processor before me. Here, surely, the only doubts would belong to philosophical scepticism. Such a judgement is obviously true. We must, in any case, allow a spectrum of cases running from those where judgements are simply true or false to where there seems no sense in such a categorical claim. Some attributions of beliefs, knowledge, motive or reason to a person are transparent. Some are radically interpretative.

Mental life is not unique in this respect. In scientific explanation we have a broad distinction between cases. There are some scientific claims which appear not to answer to any facts. Take the claim that space is Reimannian. We cannot imagine a God's eye view from which this looks like a truth in the way in which we can imagine a God's eye view from which the Bohr–Rutherford model of the atom either meets the facts or fails to do so. It is even unclear whether or not it is right to speak of it being true that space is Reimannian. So if there is a distinction to be drawn between mental life and the objects of scientific investigation along these lines, it is that the difference lies in broad similarities and dissimilarities. In general scientific practice is realist but we speak here of 'family resemblance' concepts.

Connected with this is a final and perhaps most significant way of construing the indeterminacy thesis and that is as a denial of the real essence theory of the mind held by Freud, Pears and many psychoanalysts and cognitive psychologists. There is, on this denial, no underlying set of facts which represent the way the mind runs which, viewed by the omniscient observer, would answer the question as to the way the mental facts are. Whereas the divine observer would, as I have suggested, discover the facts about the atom and confirm or refute the Bohr–Rutherford model of the atom, there is no interior to the mind, no sub-structure which contains the final answer as to whether somebody is or is not deceiving himself.

Were there underlying facts beneath the behaviour we could ask whether these facts are different from what we think them to be. Now of a single case of pain it is certainly plausible to suppose that either the person is in pain or not. The thought is that this is a matter of fact and the way those facts fall out ultimately determines the question independently of our criterion-based judgement. Is he really in pain? On the realist theory this is a matter separate from the criteria of tissue damage, writhings and avowals. Now we could imagine a situation where a consummate actor has us guessing and where we settle the issue by pointing to tissue damage etc. and arguing that if he says he is not in pain he deceives, or is even perhaps self deceiving. In this interesting way the concept of self deception can protect a criterion-based concept.

We may, contrary to the realist assumption, argue that there is no independent truth of the matter about the pain separate from our criterion-based judgement; any slack here is taken up by the introduction of self deception. What self deception does is to block the inference to ontological realism. Ontological realism would have it that there is a real fact of the matter as to whether or not the man is in pain independently of the criteria. The introduction here of the concept of self deception enables us to rest with the criteria as determining.

Let me try to explain this another way. It might seem that behaviour and tissue damage might indicate pain without my really being in pain and that I alone would know. My suggestion here is that if somebody denied he was in pain whilst exhibiting either or both these other signs we would conclude that he was self deceiving. Imagine a really strong case where somebody seems to be in agony. If his sincerity seems beyond question (he is usually truthful etc.) then we assume self deception. By this means we are able to do two things. We keep realism in its surrogate form by ensuring that outer criteria give us an answer. But we deny realism of the ontological variety by so arranging criteria and concept that nothing need be assumed about a hidden level of facts to which the sufferer alone is privy and to which the proposition 'he is in pain' ultimately corresponds. I suggest that there are no facts to turn out one way or the other over and above those which we take into account in forming our initial judgement. I would go further and claim that this also holds for intentions, motives, plans, purposes, etc. and many other concepts disjunctively required for the explanation of human action. Pain is a hard case certainly. If it is the case that somebody could be in pain without knowing that he or she is in pain, then this argument does not go through. There is a temptation to think that analgesics mask a pain which remains in existence though now concealed from consciousness. But if we take the consensus view, that to have pain is a matter of having a conscious sensation, then this argument works.

Suppose, to take another example, that a course of action on which I embark has two separate but independently sufficient reasons, one of which is altruistic and the other not. It may be better both for my department and for my wallet that I be promoted. I apply for promotion. How do I set myself to act from the good rather than the less good motive and, having acted, how do we tell which motive operated? Assume that there is nothing to suggest that one motive prevailed over the other; there are no giveaways in my talk or my behaviour. Is it the case that necessarily I acted from one rather than the other or that necessarily I acted from both? I can see no answer to this. I do not believe that there are independent facts of the matter to which my assertion either corresponds or fails to correspond.

It is important to notice that a Davidsonian view which takes motives, reasons and intentions to be causes falls foul of this feature of our mental concepts. For Davidson will have to say that there is an answer to the question. Either I acted from one or the other or my action was overdetermined. Because the relation is causal then there must be an answer to the question. The only way this is compatible with his indeterminacy is to assume that though there is an answer we may not be able to find it and that, as a matter of practice, we have either to adjudicate in an arbitrary way between criteria or admit ignorance. I think the onus of proof is on the Davidsonian to show that there exists such an answer. The admission that our concepts are not so far articulated seems to me to exclude that possibility. Given this, it seems that we can make no sense of such a claim.

The thesis is, then, that human agency requires concepts which are not resolvable in the sense of there being an essence which is how things are below the level of public observation. There is no configuration of the facts to which true propositions correspond below the level of criterial observation. Akrasia and self deception are crucial to an understanding of human nature because they point up the complexity of levels at which our desires and preferences work. What I have suggested is that in a curious way these twin concepts protect the indeterminacy of the mental by creating an illusion of a factual basis which, if it existed, would maintain realism in the mental; we then continue as though there was a level of entities in re to which our assertion answers. For self deception suggests that there is a range of facts about which the agent deceives himself and which, with uninhibited access, we might discover. Jealousy is a prime case. Here self deception paradigmatically prevents the behavioural criteria from being over-ruled by first person claims which, were they allowable, might seem to suggest privileged access to facts about the mental state. In fact, although the realism we need remains, it is now compromised by becoming surrogate or right answer realism rather than ontological realism. Indeed to take it as ontological realism would be at the price of causing the theory to collapse into logical behaviourism. On that reading, mental assertions are about behaviour rather than about something expressed in behaviour.

This surrogate for realism, as I have called it, has close relatives elsewhere in recent work on realism in morals and aesthetics. Much recent work has concentrated on finding substitutes for ontological realism which will give us the advantages of speaking as though our judgements can be true or false without the implication that a separate set of moral or aesthetic facts exists to which our judgements refer. The idea is that where realism is absent we can, as it were, create a form of ersatz realism which will serve in its stead. The role of the consensus of the qualified in the judging of the merits of a work of art allows us an objectivity about art which would otherwise seem to require that there are independent good making qualities which are criterial. Since we have not, as a matter of historical fact, been able to produce non-trivial criteria for goodness in the arts, the operation of the consensus offers us the next best thing; we can, at least, then distinguish between liking a work and thinking it good. In parallel we may be sceptical about the existence of moral qualities in re but allow that our projection of them on to the world in the way discussed by Blackburn[7] creates the illusion of objectivity. The result is, of course, anti-realism of one sort but realism of another. It is anti-realism in as much as it denies the existence of a realm of facts distinct from what our criteria recommend but realist in the sense of allowing a right answer subject to the proviso that a means exists whereby a consensus can be established as to what is right or wrong. I have expressed reservations earlier about the assumption of moral determinacy. My thesis as far as mental predicates is concerned is that talk of the mind is nearly always non-realist with respect to underlying structures and quite often non-realist with respect to offering answers to questions. It exhibits both ontological non-realism and surrogate non-realism.

If the Cartesian view were correct and we knew our own minds better than anything else and better than anybody else's, then any clash between the deliverances of introspection and the behavioural evidence would be resolved in favour of the inner source. There would be no reason to believe that the normal form of self deception could occur for Cartesianism makes that form of self deception which is recognised by others impossible. There would be an inner truth about the matter which could be reached and which would represent the facts of the matter. Furthermore I would be in a uniquely privileged position to reach this truth. This is quite incompatible with the view expressed here that the role of self deception can be to moderate between inner and outer in such a way as to permit the outer to have the final say. At least one form of realism, the idea that there is an inner state in which resides the right answer to questions about motivation, desires, etc., is undermined by the existence of self deception. If there was such an inner reality, introspection would give us access.

There are, indeed, conflicting demands on our concept of the mind. We need as much determinacy as we can muster for the application of concepts. We cannot learn to apply the correlative language unless there is a broad bond between what we all say. The move towards surrogate realism becomes readily intelligible. Without it, it is difficult to see how linguistic ascriptions will be possible. On the other hand there is no doubt that the freedom of interpretation marks out a significant human value. It enables us to view our fellow men with charity by placing the best construction on their actions; it helps us to be less hard on ourselves as well. It is not an unmixed evil nor an unqualified good.

II

There is another important feature of the way in which we talk about persons for which the Lockean conception of real essences seems to provide a model. We think of some of a person's characteristics as being deep and others as being superficial. Another way of presenting the distinction is to speak of the real President Bush as opposed to the surface. The Freudian apparatus of ego, superego and id provides one way of handling this. Freud thinks of the ego as the real self, beset by the demands of id and superego. The Freudian ontology does preserve the distinction between the deep and surface levels of the personality, a distinction crucial to the extension of the Lockean model to the human sciences. If the Freudian is, in some ways, the paradigm of those unsound ontologies which treat the human mind on a systemic basis, the model has ancient roots. Bruno Snell[8] argued that Heraclitus was the first thinker to speak of the mind as having depth and as possessing its own space. Previously Greek talk of the mind had been in terms of an analogy with physical organs.

Freud's favoured analogy of archaeology is, in some respects, appropriate, though what archaeology discovers is inert whereas the Freudian is essentially a dynamic theory of the mind. The germ theory of disease or the Brownian motion were, no doubt, the models Freud and his contemporaries had in mind. But the paradigm is quite pervasive. In music the most influential of modern analysts, Heinrich Schenker, quite explicitly distinguishes surface and depth, the deep analysis exhibiting a structure which the surface conceals; elsewhere we have the Marxist distinction between base and superstructure and Chomskyan transformational grammars. It is easy to be swept away and find the contrast in all sorts of areas. Aside from the obvious models of Freud and Marx, Lévi-Strauss cites geology[9] as formative in his intellectual development because geology reveals a structure below the surface. The pattern does seem to be pervasive in modern culture. Now, since deep interpretation *a fortiori* shares the features of ordinary interpretation, we are faced with the problem of making sense of the idea of deep interpretation while acknowledging that the model of realism in science is misleading. The concepts associated with deep interpretation are concepts like 'illusion', 'deception', 'unmasking', 'disclosing', 'unveiling', 'uncovering' and 'transforming'. Something is concealed, whether deliberately or not, and interpretation discloses it. It is easy to see how naturally we slip into the realist model. I am going to suggest that deep interpretation differs in that the analyst, whilst using the methods of paratactic and thematic analysis, also takes an extra step. Until they are translated, the Freudian symbols in dreams do not yield their meaning or their significance. He has to decode in such a way that, when transformed, the themes can be seen to be connected with the surface. Neurotic rituals, especially, have to be decoded in order to see the connection with waking life. Schenker's ur-linie may not bear any immediately recognizable relation to the music whose structure it explains. It has to be transformed by the addition of notes, by transposition or by rhythmic alterations. The elements which are reached through deep interpretation are not what the ordinary non-specialist onlooker, listener or reader would immediately recognise as features of the object. There is no routine procedure which gives depth interpretation.

I am not going to argue that this is other than a vague and basically epistemic criterion, but it is probably as clear as the topic allows. Although 'deep interpretation' is not a term of art in literary theory, Traversi's argument that *The Winter's Tale*[10] is about reconciliation strikes me as about as clear an example of deep interpretation as we are likely to get. The word 'reconciliation' does not appear in Shakespeare's text. We have to make the connections.

There is another way of making the distinction between real and apparent or between depth and surface traits in a personality which has received attention recently; it is by distinguishing those of my desires and motives which I approve of in myself, or endorse, and those which seem to be extraneous to me, those desires which seem to me to be less integrated with the person I am, desires which impinge upon me and which I cannot reconcile with the rest of my wishes and projects. These are desires which though I cannot simply suppress or ignore still seem external to me. Thus a sudden access of jealousy may be so untypical of me as to seem more something which happens to me than something which belongs to me. Such desires do not count as reasons for actions. I would not want to act upon them and would not think that there is any pressure to do so.

An analogy is perhaps in the thoughts which occur to me rather than are thought by me in the fullest sense. There is a difference between those thoughts I incorporate in what I am now writing and the way in which the thought of an accident comes back to haunt me, rising unbidden into my consciousness. Indeed a particularly terrifying nightmare is the prospect of no longer being able to control one's thoughts so that associations, ideas and thoughts race through the mind in an internally disconnected way immune to the will. For normally, as Diderot put it, 'Mes pensées sont mes catins.' Penelhum and Frankfurt[11] describe such unprompted thoughts and desires as external rather than internal. Further along the spectrum still are those desires whose externality is beyond question, desires which arise from post-hypnotic suggestion, for example. It is also worth noting that amongst the desires which I disown will be many desires which are so insistent that I am not free to deny them. Some of the desires which I reject are desires which I cannot control and the behaviour which I wish to reject is behaviour which I cannot avoid even though I do it. Jealousy, falling in love, remorse and lust all have these features of apparent externality. They vary in the way in which they seem external. Sometimes they fail to fit in with my other desires; sometimes they are desires which, although they 'fit in', I do not endorse; sometimes they may just seem abnormal. But despite the fact that these 'happen to us' they may also be characteristic. Somebody may know that she is the sort of person who falls precipitately in love, not wish to, and yet recognise, rather glumly, that this is how she is. She may also glory in her frailty. Our attitudes to overmastering emotions are often complex.

In a sense, of course, these desires are still mine. It is I who want them satisfied and I may be responsible for the actions which follow. I may even predict their onset whilst doing nothing to place myself in the position which enables me to satisfy them when they do arise. Their external nature is shown not by the fact that I predict their occurrence; I can, after all, predict that I shall be hungry in four hours without my wishing to repudiate that desire; it is rather by the fact that in the cases of desires I endorse, I make provision now, if provision is appropriate. Thus I may ensure there is food in the house. But if I did not want to satisfy the desire I might place myself in a position where I could not satisfy it and there is no truer test of the externality of the desire. I try to head it off. An alcoholic may deliberately make sure that he is miles from drink or a smoker who wishes to kick the habit may make sure that he has no cigarettes available the next time he needs one. A schoolmaster who taught Richard Dawkins was prone to sudden and uncontrollable rages and when driven beyond endurance by his pupils would shout: 'Take cover, I feel it coming on.'

One feature of persons, as opposed to members of other species, is that they can evaluate and either accede to or inhibit their own desires, a thesis most notably advanced by Harry Frankfurt[12] in a series of recent papers. I may want to have a drink. If, however, I fear alcoholism, I will not want to have that desire. There seems no reason to think that other mammals are capable of this sort of reflection on their first order desires. They are what Frankfurt calls 'wantons'; they are merely the prey of their desires. We, however, can say with St Paul, 'That which I would not do, that I do';[13] this sounds implausible if said of a dog.

In the case I have described, St Paul apparently reflects on his loss of freedom in handling his desires. The desire moves him to act, though he does not want either to have that desire or to act upon it. Sometimes we are the victim of our desires; the sad cases of sexual offenders paraded in court often testify to this. But many of us can resist our desires. I would like that second biscuit, but I am trying to lose weight. I do not wish to act on that desire and I refrain from doing so. There are such cases where I both wish to

51

act upon the desire, wish not to and wish I did not have the desire. There are also occasions where one may be pleased to have the desire but not wish to act upon it. Sexual attraction may be enjoyable qua desire, even if one recognises that the costs of acting upon it are too great.

Of course, the judgement of a friend or of somebody else who knows me well as to whether this desire and the action which matches it is out of sorts with my real self is likely to be less exclusive of possibilities than my own. Penelhum recognises this in as much as he recognises the role that self deception may play in these cases. If I am given *carte blanche* to reject desires as external, the opportunities for self exculpation become too considerable.

Whilst recognizing the role played by these features of persons which require, first and foremost, a distinction between first and second order desires, between wanting something and wanting the desire itself, we might consider a second way of distinguishing the real and apparent features of an individual. This is the distinction between the evanescent and the permanent, a distinction which has made a distinctive contribution to intellectual history. A modern version is to be found in Penelhum who argues that self identity comes when the desires by which I am moved are those which I wish to move me. Some desires which impinge upon me, sudden bizarre yearnings, or desires which are implanted through drugs, electrodes, or post-hypnotic suggestion are desires which I will regard as external to me in a way and such desires are relatively impermanent. One reason for distinguishing these would be the causal route they take. We might wish to say that the causal origins of normal desires are non deviant in a way in which these are not. However, there are good reasons for resisting this sort of account. Deviant causal paths are a topic which has been much discussed of late but I think that, in this context, the explanation lies elsewhere. Even if we could find a satisfactory analysis of deviancy which was neither circular nor *ad hoc*, the analysis is remote from the way the distinction functions. For the point is not the difference of origin but the fact that these desires are desires which I do not endorse and, more particularly, they are desires which are discontinuous with my understanding of my situation and myself, to put it into Frankfurt's words.

Certainly, the externalisation which comes from rejecting a desire as not part of my identity may have to be revoked in the light of experience. I may come to find that certain desires which I thought were extraneous are really permanent aspects of my personality with which I must come to grips. A passion which I admit to myself to be dangerous or evil may have to be channelled into less harmful areas, perhaps through indulging it in fantasy. A man given to perverse or violent impulses may first of all reject these as external to himself, as mere visitations. With dawning self knowledge he realises that these desires are both too frequent and come too readily to be dismissed in this way.

We tend to regard those passions which arise too frequently for comfort as genuine and real parts of the personality. We may dismiss sporadic passions as external; we cannot do this with those which arise frequently. Even their unbiddenness suggests their 'reality'. Desires which arise frequently in this way are desires which we will regard as 'permanent' rather than ephemeral. Permanence, together with considerations of consistency and predictability enable me to pick out those desires which are part of me as opposed to those which are extraneous.

I suspect that the intuitive understanding we have of the distinction between deep and superficial is a mixture of various considerations and there seems no good reason for supposing it to be clearly definable. Our everyday understanding of the distinction may, quite possibly, be muddled and there certainly will not be grounds for supposing that the distinction lies in a clear form in our pre-analytic understanding and that it is only our theoretical understanding of it which is muddled. There is no reason to think that we make, in practice, perfectly clear distinctions and that it is only when we come to theorise about them that confusion ensues. The ambiguities lie, I suspect, in the nature of the things. All we can say is that there are various ways of making the distinction between deep and surface traits of the character.

How do we arrive at demotic assessments of character? The answer I have proposed in this study is that it is a form of interpretative thematic analysis, involving paratactic dissection of the narrative flow of our life but not requiring any assumptions about underlying causal processes. Later I attempt to analyse akrasia and self deception in these terms. Of course, we have to allow that people differ greatly in the degree to which they conceal their real motives or prevailing interests. Some are much more complex and devious than others. In all cases, the narrative analysis somehow has to match the way we acquire knowledge of the individual. In other words, there has to be a match between the assessment we make of a personality and the thematic analysis which produces it. With a person who is easily understood, the salient features, the features which are connected to the bulk of his or her behaviour are obvious; they protrude. So if envy is a dominant motive, that envy may be easily recognisable by expression, reaction and behaviour. The envy appears often; he or she is envious of many people and on many occasions. The behaviour which he or she displays may often be plausibly explained as caused by or motivated by envy. A complex person whose behaviour conceals or misleads may also be envious but his or her behaviour is not easy to interpret simply because he or she dissembles. The salient features of his or her behaviour may be more disputable, more matters on which people will differ and on which the difference is a consequence of broader differences in moral outlook. Hence it may be less easy to see when he or she acts in character. This parallels the difference between an obvious and a controversial interpretation of a work of art.

In saying this I do not wish to give the impression that the character thus assessed through interpretative procedures has no causal role to play in the production of the behaviour which expresses it. As I have said elsewhere, I do not think the causality involved is like the causality of the physical processes. There is a parallel in the arts; there is no reason why what is discovered to be a theme in a work of art should not, presumably through unconscious means, play a part in creating the aesthetic surface.

III

The next problem is the extension of this analysis to the question of self knowledge. We do not want self knowledge to display quite different features from our knowledge of others. There must be connections between my self knowledge and the knowledge that others have of me. If, for example, it turns out that self knowledge is conveniently analysable on the model of real essences we shall once again be left with a split between two forms of knowledge of the mind, one for the first person case and one for second and third person. Such a gap produces intolerable problems in the acquisition of the language of the mind, as we have learnt from Wittgenstein. We must have a connection between the way we learn our concepts and their application to ourselves.

Self knowledge covers a variety of cases. We can dismiss cases such as my knowledge that I am under six feet tall as of no special interest. These are not instances of self knowledge proper. But in the area with which we are concerned there might seem a fairly sharp distinction between knowledge of feelings such as pain and that form of self knowledge which involves propositional attitudes such as beliefs and desires. In some cases, it is said, I have privileged access to my own mental states and in some cases not. For example, it is argued that I am so far in the best position to recognise that I am in pain that if I am over-ruled on the basis of behavioural evidence by a second party, then it follows that I must have been insincere or self deceiving in denying that I am in pain, always assuming that pain is taken to be a mental state. (Churchland[14] has an excellent counter example: a captured spy expects to be tortured; instead of a red hot poker being applied to his back, he has an ice cube; but for a moment he thinks he is in pain. From the fact that he thinks he is in pain it does not follow that he really is.) Equally, intentions are also an area in which the agent is especially able to determine the mental facts. As I showed earlier in this chapter, the role of self deception is such that it gives behavioural facts the chance of dominance over any internal revelations or first person claims. Indeed, the force of the arguments I present suggests that privileged access is essentially unimportant in the structure of our concepts for its role is marginal, isolated or neutralised.

In these important cases, my grasp of the nature of my own personality may depend on the same behavioural clues as others require. I have the advantage, of course, of being my own constant companion and this partly accounts for the impression of privileged access. But it only explains it in part; setting aside sensations such as pain, whose 'mental status' is not clear, we have another group of mental phenomena to which we have, it seems, privileged access and these are our aims, intentions and purposes. The making of these is, without doubt, a form of action. I act when I form an intention and I act when I recall, imagine, remember or formulate something in my mind. The knowledge I have of these is similar to the knowledge I have of my other actions; after all if I did not believe that I was calculating the square root of 256 I would set about doing something different from what I am doing much as if I did not think I was driving to work I would change my route. I shall say more of this in chapter three. Still, in other cases where motivation is more complex and where a variety of considerations are involved we can understand that self knowledge requires the same sort of thematic understanding as I use in assessing the motives and mental life of my fellow men.

An essentialist account of the self will naturally tend to see such self knowledge as a species of causal knowledge. Churchland explicitly espouses this view. Now, since there is a reasonably well understood causal pathway connecting damaged tissue to the brain, we might regard pain as an apt case for a causal analysis. But it is not possible to conceive that there are unfelt pains (or, more precisely, the question is not an empirical question but a matter for more or less trivial conceptual decision). This, transparently, is not the case with respect to emotions, motives, moods or personal traits. I can be jealous without knowing, even though it is obvious to others. But the assessment of such states is frequently interpretative.

The point can be made in the form of a fork. Either my aims, intentions, etc. are what I formulate and are therefore conscious because they are actions of mine or they are discoverable from an analysis of patterns of behaviour. I note how I react to opportunities, for example. Now in the latter case (which is interpretative), the agent is not privileged. I am no better, possibly even worse, at estimating my motives than the onlooker. The only advantage I have is that I am always present at my undertakings. But in neither case is the knowledge of a causal form. In the first case there is no room for a contingent relation between object and knowledge; in the second there is no determination of the interpretation by what is interpreted in such a way as to match the standard form of the causal connection. All that one can say here, and this is unobjectionable, is that the object of interpretation is a causal factor in the production of the interpretation but its causal role is necessarily less extensive than in the standard case of my knowing that, for example, I sit before a word processor.

Notice that we do not say of somebody who knows that he is in pain that he has self knowledge on that account. The man who knows himself sees himself as others see him. His view of himself is free from flattery or self deception. Of course, although self deception most commonly occludes self knowledge, laziness or inattention may also play a part; however, the importance of self deception here underlines Hamlyn's remark that valuation seems built into self knowledge.[15] This in itself will raise doubts about the appropriateness of the causal model here. And yet a degree of determination is required by the way in which deception assumes that certain facts about the person are set and are, in consequence, what the self deceiver fails to grasp. There is, in fact, a way in which self knowledge can be both knowledge of relatively determined facts and yet narrative and interpretative in form. There are some descriptions of what I do which are not in dispute. What I said on a particular occasion may be given a description with which different observers may agree even though they may disagree, and we could imagine the disagreement to be irresolvable, as to whether what was done counts as an act of self interest or an act of statesmanship. Many political actions are ambiguous in this way. Indeed, for there to be a disagreement there must be some common ground which is the locus of disagreement and without this it is impossible to see what sense could be attached to the claim that interpretation is underdetermined.

Two considerations militate against this picture. They both suggest a move in the direction of determinacy, though without that goal being attained. First my behaviour may converge upon the character which I ascribe to myself. I have an image of myself which may have a regulative function and I may endeavour to make my character converge upon this self image. I shall have more to say about the ingredients of this in the penultimate chapter. The crucial point here is that if we concede that understanding is interpretative and thus underdetermined, we do not preclude a relative and progressive determinacy in the object of that knowledge. In this way the interpretation of persons is unlike the interpretation of the arts because nothing much like this seems to happen in the arts. Only an aesthetic idealist who believes that the real work of art is constituted by the current critical understanding or the current best critical understanding or some such account could maintain that the work of art progressively changes under the guiding influence of a chosen interpretation. Interpretation does seem to me to be paradigmatically a family resemblance concept and one or more marks of standard interpretation may be absent without our wishing to say that we no longer have interpretation. But we must, I think, conclude that the role of agency means that the processes of narrative selection and narrative construction do not apply to the single individual in quite the way they apply elsewhere. The individual can attempt to manufacture a consistency in his own life which means that his behaviour will then stem from a predictable and intelligible base. We can create a personality in which various features are salient; the alternative may be a personality which lacks integration. Perhaps it is worth pointing out that the role of agency brings, in this way, the planning of life closer to the planning of art. The artist may create a whole whose parts interconnect so that the various elements conspire to bring about the character of the whole. Subsequently the thematically important features of the personality may come to cause directly some of the behaviour with which they are connected without there being any longer any deliberation on the part of the agent.

The second way in which interpretations of the individual character may converge on determinacy is the way in which our judgement of episodes may be controlled by our assessment of character. The thought is this; if we think that a person is, say, excessively controlled, then we may take an outburst by him to be a devious means of manipulating his audience rather than simply temper. If, on the other hand, we think of somebody as spontaneous we might dismiss the thought that a particular action is contrived. In this way we have what we could describe as a top-down picture of the relation of character to individual actions. A broad asessment of character may enable us to cancel our judgement of individual episodes. The temptation is to think that there is a fact of the matter, that either the reaction was contrived or it was not. Much of my argument in this chapter has been against the general validity of this sort of realism. If my arguments are correct, at least one form of determinacy with respect to the mental is excluded and this is the form which rests mental events on an underlying sub-structure which causes them to have the features they do. In addition that variety of determinism is ruled out which holds that the behaviour which seems to us to be paradigmatically free is, in fact, the product of and constrained by events at a lower level. Of course, it does not touch a determinism which is sequential in a Humean way, resting the occurrence of present events on events which occurred earlier, nor does it exclude a determinism which rests on a mind–brain identity.

The point again is, I believe, that we have another way in which realism, here identified with determinacy, can be manufactured, this time through the actions of the agent whose behaviour we investigate. For we can imagine constructing a situation such that there is, after all, in general, a right answer to the question we put to the world about our mental life. The difference is now that we create the facts which correspond to the attribution – it is a case of 'making an honest proposition' out of the situation. There is, perhaps, one final comment to be made. Some of the harder cases are cases where it is uncertain whether we should say we are making a moral judgement or a judgement of fact about the mind. 'Do I really want to do that?'; 'Do I really love her?'. We may certainly say that any hesitation we have over making such judgements, which may superficially seem to be questions about the facts, is due to the realisation of the moral implications of the assessment. A positive answer demands action from me. I may be asking myself rather obliquely whether I should permit these desires and attitudes to flourish and that certainly is a moral issue. Even somebody tempted by moral realism will agree that there may be no right answer to such questions. Even the moral realist does not have to be a realist all the time.

3

THE IDEA OF A FOLK
PSYCHOLOGY

In some respects this central chapter is an interlude in the argument of the book. It is more closely argued than much of the rest and readers whose interest in philosophy is not professional may wish to skip it. But it is, I believe, necessary to confront a view which has a deal of backing amongst philosophers, a sort of universally acknowledged cliché; it is that our ordinary mental predicates form a a proto-scientific theory of the mind, a theory which takes mental entities to form an inner mechanism or essence. Obviously this is not a view I can accept consistently with what I have argued earlier and I shall attack it on a very broad front by denying that folk psychology, as it is described, is a theory at all. As I have intimated, philosophers with a yen for conceptual reform are nowadays prone to describe our ordinary, common sense, Rylean description of the mind as 'folk psychology', the implication being that when we ascribe intentions, beliefs, motives and emotions to others we are offering explanations of that person's behaviour, explanations which belong to a sort of pre-scientific theory. Though the term is in vogue, the philosophers whose belief in folk psychology make their writings very acceptable clay pigeons are Paul and Patricia Churchland and Stich.[1] All three contrast folk psychology with a pukka theory about the mind and its workings which is either broadly materialist or more specifically based on the computer model. For all three, folk psychology is thought of as a Stone Age relative of more respectable scientific theories. For all three, folk psychology is as theoretical an enterprise as the explanation of the reflex contraction of the pupil in the face of a bright light in terms of a neural network. The origin of these ideas seems to lie in Wilfred Sellars's work of a couple of decades ago;[2] I shall argue that our policy should be *caveat emptor.*

The philosophical connections of this issue are considerable. Philosophers who believe that explanation in the physical sciences is the model for understanding in general tend to regard common sense explanations as successful to the extent that they converge on the scientific model. There is then a motive for thinking of common sense explanations as rivals to more creditable scientific theories.

What is somewhat surprising is that those philosophers who have used the idea have not stopped to ask whether the attribution of beliefs etc. shows the characteristics of theory explanation. I shall argue that in some respects 'mental statements' have the characteristics of theoretical explanations whilst in other ways they are not theory-like. I find myself, then, midway between Churchland on the one hand who thinks that common sense ascription of mental predicates is unambiguously theoretical and Kathy Wilkes[3] who denies that we have a prescientific theory of the mind. But I shall also try to show that the way in which mental statements are theory-like is of no use to those philosophers like Stich and the Churchlands who either wish to replace folk psychology with a more respectable scientific alternative or who think that this is an option for us. Quite the reverse. The theoretical form of statements about the mind actually places insuperable obstacles in the way of a replacement of folk psychology by a computational or neurological alternative.

The Churchlands take our attribution of beliefs to persons to posit causal relationships between psychological states or events and the behaviour which these explain. So when I use the practical syllogism to explain why a man is signing his name I point out that it is a cheque which he is signing and that he believes that if he signs this bit of paper he thereby purchases the book he desires. So the action is explained by postulating a desire and a belief. The theory can be generalised to provide a set of universal statements which give a theory of the inner dynamics of human beings and which contain detailed hypotheses about the determinants of human behaviour; hypotheses which enable us to explain and predict.

Paul Churchland also thinks that this theory is deficient in many ways. First, it gives very inadequate accounts of the dynamics of emotions, creativity, perceptual illusion, differences in intelligence or of mental illness. Second, and perhaps more significantly, it has shown no improvement in millenia. Third, it assumes a discontinuity between the mental life of infants, animals and ourselves which is obviously false. For a fourth and final charge against folk psychology I turn again to Stich. Phenomena like cognitive dissonance show the unsatisfactory nature of folk psychology.[4]

Some of these charges can be quickly dismissed. Common sense makes attributions of emotions and beliefs to animals and infants without any great difficulty. Irrationality of the sort displayed in akrasia, cognitive dissonance or self deception is hardly to be laid at the door of the common sense theory of the mind. We would need some general grounds for supposing that the failings are to be placed at the feet of the theory rather than at those of the individual concerned. Behind this may be the suspicion that if self deception is so widespread as to be endemic then the conclusion ought to be that we have our theory wrong. But, of course, these forms of irrationality are not so widespread as to be excluded on the basis of Davidsonian arguments. In any case, like the blunderbuss use of the principle of charity or humanity, this ignores what is peculiarly human about inconsistency, the desire not to hurt or be hurt, to deal gently with other people as well as to present yourself, to yourself and others, in the best light.

We need to start by considering, however briefly and inadequately, what it is for something to be a theory. The paradigms of theories for our age are, of course, those to be found in the physical sciences: the kinetic theory of gases, Newtonian mechanics, the general theory of relativity or the chemical theory of valency are examples. In old fashioned textbooks on the philosophy of science we find them presented as though they are hypotheses from which the phenomena they explain may be deduced. Of course, theories do not have to take this form. A theory which does not entail what it purports to explain or whose laws are not really 'laws' may still be a theory and, though flawed, may, through these very flaws, prove highly fertile as the subject develops. It is interesting to note, however, that the deductive paradigm for theoretical explanation has at least one parallel in action, and that is in practical inference; here we connect belief and desire with action through the practical syllogism. Looking away from natural science, consider Moore's theory of ethics. Again we describe it as a theory even though its disparate ingredients, the non-natural theory of the good, its consequentialism and its enumeration of the paramount goods are not deductively integrated nor is there anything remotely resembling a law of nature. What these cases have in common is that they explain in a generalisable way. A theory does not have to be general; a historian may have a specific hypothesis about a specific event or action. But scientific explanations, and these are the model for Stich and the Churchlands, are general. For these writers, the model of physical theory is the paradigm of what a scientific theory will be like. So in what ensues it must be remembered that folk psychology is thought to explain in the way that atomic theory explains. The idea is that of an internal mechanism which accounts for behavioural phenomena through its nature and structure. They offer 'hidden mechanism' forms of explanation. To summarise, then, we explain discrete bits of behaviour by postulating desires, wants, beliefs, etc. on the part of the agent. But in order to do this we require generalisations of a rather vague sort. Paul Churchland lists such banalities as 'Persons who are angry tend to frown', 'Persons who are angry tend to be impatient' and 'Persons who are deprived of fluids tend to feel thirst'. Patricia Churchland suggests 'barring a stronger impulse, hunger causes eating' and 'barring stimulants or desperate purposes, weariness causes sleep'. We are then able to explain behaviour so that we can say of a person that he or she wants a drink not for the sake of sociability but because he or she is thirsty.

Now one very important question which has a bearing on the criticisms I shall make later is whether all our talk of mind is folk psychological in this way or whether only some of it is. Stich is unclear;[5] he describes folk psychology as evolving as an aid to our dealings one with another. Paul Churchland is unequivocal.[6] Since folk psychology is simultaneously a solution to the problem of other minds it seems clear that all mental ascriptions are folk psychological and that consequently all our accounts of other minds are theory-facilitated. The general idea, astounding when presented in this way, seems to be that I ask myself why it is that bits of the world keep bumping uncomfortably against me. Is it perhaps because I keep treading on parts of the world? I then formulate the hypothesis that treading on bits of the world makes those bits angry and the anger results in reprisals against me. By a process of refinement we eventually reach the explanation that Smith hits me because I annoy him by standing on his toe. In what follows I shall assume the stronger version, that all mental ascriptions are folk psychological, not just because Churchland subscribes to it, but also because the weaker theory is neither interesting nor controversial. It would, after all, hardly surprise us to learn that people sometimes formulate theories about other people in terms of ordinary talk about the mind, nor that some of the concepts we use originate in theorising. Indeed I shall say more about the latter towards the end.

Now to the first of the three criticisms which I propose to make of folk psychology theory. I have privileged access to some of my mental states and of these I can offer direct self revelation. There is an antique flavour to this claim; nevertheless I think it is, fortunately, true. I sometimes have thoughts, even during a philosophy seminar, which I am relieved to know are not transparent. I am making no claim to the incorrigibility which is usually associated with the idea of privileged access, incidentally. Of course, I may postulate a belief on the part of an agent as a means of explaining what he does but he may also tell me. He can explain his behaviour to me and he can do so because, in many cases, he knows straight off what he believes and the role his belief plays in his action. He has privileged access to his belief and I learn of it through his direct self revelation. Certainly there are cases where I do not know why I do something but cases of self deception or illusion are a minority. It is easy, in the interests of stressing the similarity between mental and physical explanations, to do what Churchland does, and exaggerate the number and importance of these quasi-pathological cases. If the reader feels as uncomfortable as I do about the idea of privileged access then he is welcome to translate the discussion into terms less immediately perspicuous but less burdened with Cartesianism. We need only remark that many attributions to ourselves are not explanations.

This is an issue much discussed by believers in folk psychology. But its real force has not been appreciated. For the point about these cases of privileged access as far as the folk psychological thesis is concerned is the following. Amongst the mental states to which I have privileged access are mental states which apparently play no role in the explanation of behaviour and which are certainly not postulated in the way that Churchland and other advocates of the existence of a folk psychology suggest. For example, I find, when playing the piano, that all sorts of fragmentary memories of places flit across my mind in a way I cannot account for. All of us probably have this experience of suddenly recalling people or places apparently *ex nihilo*. Though there may be an explanation as to why I recall in this way, there does not have to be and I may not know what it is. However this may be it does seem that nothing is explained by these memories even if there is in turn an explanation of why I have them. What folk psychological theorists have to assume is that their existence is required to explain behaviour. I suppose that their existence explains the criticism I am currently making of Churchland and Stich but it is somewhat preposterous to suggest that their existence is postulated to make possible a criticism of Professors Stich and Churchland. Normally they are simply unconnected intrusions into the stream of my mental life. They are, in truth, more like brute facts than bits of theory and this is something that the other side does not seem to recognise. For believers in a folk psychological theory the facts are bits of behaviour and what explains these facts are the hypothesised mental states.

An objection which has much the same force and structure uses the case of qualia. Phenomenologically my experience of blue is different from my experience of red though if there were a reversal of the spectrum so that what looks blue looks red and vice versa, there need be no behavioural consequences. This is disputed and so for this reason, and also because of the size of the literature it has generated, I do not propose to place much emphasis on it here. But if you think that there is a case for taking qualia to be unconnected with behaviour then their existence is a counter example for believers in the existence of a folk psychology in as much as the nature of qualia cannot explain behaviour; only the distinction between them does that. Again, even though the existence of qualia has at least one behavioural consequence, namely the writing of philosophical articles about them, it would be ludicrous to say that their existence was postulated to explain that chunk of behaviour.

Needless to say, the concept of behaviour is not itself a demotic one. It is worth pointing out just how much philosophical sophistication is presumed in the hypothesis of a folk psychology. In order to set up the explanation of behaviour by recourse to inner mental states we need a Cartesian distinction between behaviour and the mind. Normally scientific theories do not require such philosophically loaded points of origin. We may assume that ordinary scientific theories can be expressed in any one of a number of ontologies. For example, it is always assumed that Newtonian theory can be expressed in a realist or in a phenomenalist metaphysics. It is, indeed, difficult to think of a case of a scientific theory which not only originates in a discredited philosophical theory – many do that – but could not get off the ground without the philosophical assumptions. The philosophy is never essential to the framing of the scientific theory though it may be, contingently, its point of origin. Science is invariant with respect to philosophical presuppositions. That this is not the case with respect to an imagined folk psychology is a strong reason for suspecting its scientific credentials.

Having seen one way in which some mental statements are unlike theoretical postulates and more like statements of observation, let us look at a way in which they are more like bits of theory. It is a commonplace that much mental talk is intensional. Motives, desires, emotions, wishes and intentions have objects. If I am afraid there is something of which I am afraid; if I have an intention, then it is an intention to do something specific; there is something which I intend to accomplish; if I remember, then there is something which I remember and so on. There is a further feature which might be marked by speaking of contents rather than objects. Mental states incorporate contents in the sense that we speak of beliefs as having contents. 'Incorporate' covers a multitude of sins here; I shall try to do something to redeem it later on. For the moment allow that if I desire something then I believe that that thing has properties which make it desirable. If I fear something then that object has properties which, in my belief, make it dangerous. All this, of course, must be qualified by the observation that my beliefs about them may be mistaken. I can fear a perfectly inoffensive dog.

Next we need to note that the identity of these mental states will involve component objects. We discriminate hopes, fears, beliefs and intentions in terms of their objects; this desire is different from that desire in virtue of what it is a desire for. So although I have a multiplicity of desires at any one time, their discrimination is possible because of their different objects; I both want to get this argument straight and want a cup of coffee. Some of my desires are short term and some long term. Now there are no phenomenological features of the desire which enable me to pick it out; they do not feel different; they differ in their objects and in the strength which I feel them to have. But their mode of existence is that they have objects; change the object and you change the desire. Consequently the scope for describing the same desire in different terms is extremely limited. Although it would be a bit imprecise to say that if you change the description you change the desire which is thereby designated, it is not far from the truth. The point about desires is that they are identified and individuated by us under specific descriptions and that is their mode of existence.

When we act we typically act in the belief that something or other will be brought about; there are exceptions but for the sake of this argument they do not matter since we are essentially interested in constructing counter examples. Actions are defined in terms of what, to borrow a term from aesthetics, may be called their history of production; the difference between sticking my arm out of the window to stretch and sticking it out to acknowledge a friend lies in the intention with which I do it. But intentions have objects and without this feature I cannot distinguish them. Qua movements they may be indistinguishable. Qua actions they are distinguished in terms of my intention in doing them. In the case of actions the history of production is part of the way in which we individuate that action. Without it we may be unable to distinguish one action from another. More seriously, and this is the crucial consideration, viewed as behaviour alone, we have no reason to discriminate them. Not until we distinguish them have we any reason to explain one differently from the other. In order to distinguish them, and to offer different explanations, we have to regard them as actions and not as mere bodily movements. What this shows, of course, is that we have to presume the concepts of intention, purpose, etc., themselves mental concepts, in order to individuate the objects of explanation.

So an important interim conclusion is this.

1 Folk psychology is thought to postulate mental states such as intentions to explain behaviour.
2 But behaviour once thus explained is action.
3 Action incorporates intentions and is individuated on that basis.
4 Consequently the account offered would make the folk psychological enterprise question-begging. We need 'mental' states in order to distinguish the things which they are introduced to explain.

I want to develop this objection a little further. I have argued that two bits of behaviour may be indistinguishable without drawing on the apparatus of 'mental concepts' which we require for their explanation. But, moreover, the boundaries we draw between one bit of behaviour and another we draw on the basis of that mental content which is embodied in these bits when viewed as action. To put it more crudely: how do we chop up behaviour into explanation-sized bites? We take a whole sentence and not a sentence and a half as the locus of explanation; if our interest was purely in the phenomena qua neurological occurrence, then there is no reason why we should draw the bounds where we do. The criteria for taking a group of neural events together need not be the same. We do so on the unacknowledged assumption that we are dealing with actions. We are again left with the objection that folk psychological theory requires us to assume the theory in order to discriminate the objects which it has been introduced to explain.

In order to ease the passage of the next stage in my argument I assume further that many actions are performed in the belief that they are actions of a type. They incorporate beliefs much as they incorporate intentions. Consequently if what folk psychology is explaining is human action then part of what is explained will be content. It is characteristic of many actions that when doing them I believe that that is what I am doing when I am doing it. This is particularly evident when the action involves a process like driving to work. If I intended to drive to work but did not believe that I was on the right road then I would alter my action accordingly. My belief, as well as my intention, distinguishes my taking a car for a test drive as opposed to a pleasure trip, for instance. Beliefs, in many cases, 'track' actions. This is not simply a contingency. It is necessary, not just that I have the intention to drive to work, but also that I believe that I am doing so in order that it counts as driving to work. There would be an inconsistency in the idea that I intend that I now be driving to work whilst believing that I am not doing so. How I individuate my action depends upon the accompanying belief just as it depends upon the related intention.

These considerations may seem grist to the mill of those who think of beliefs as theoretical entities. 'This falling body is under gravitational attraction' is not the same as 'This body is seeking its natural location' even though, at least for realists, both describe the same phenomenon, one description couched in Newtonian theory and the other in Aristotelian. The difference between them seems analogous to the difference in content between distinct beliefs for, again, identity depends upon content.

However, beliefs present special problems for the advocate of eliminative materialism. As we have seen, where replacement by another theory is possible the same entity has to be described in terms of a fresh theory. But if the identity conditions for beliefs are as I have said, then virtually no other description is possible which individuates the same entity. What I believe must be expressed in the terms which register the content of the belief. Expressed in other terms we have another possible or actual belief or perhaps no belief at all. So the theoretical form of beliefs presents insuperable obstacles in the way of replacement. Another way of putting the same point is to say that there is an essentialist description of thoughts. Their content is such that only one way of understanding them is possible. So when, for instance, Freud tells us that a thought of the Queen is really a thought of one's mother he has not said anything intelligible. Of course, there may be ways of teasing out the significance of this idea but taken *in strictu sensu*, one cannot make anything of it.

Note that there is no exit here via any fancy ideas about incommensurability. Those who think they see a folk psychology are adamant that it makes sense to ask whether computational psychology or neurological theory are improvements on folk psychology, so they cannot accept that these alternatives are not rivals between themselves and with folk psychology. An improved theory must, amongst its conditions, explain the same phenomena as the old theory even if its scope overlaps with the previous incumbent rather than being coextensive with it. So we are then required to identify the facts that folk psychology explains. Churchland seems to have no doubt that these facts are bits of human behaviour. Thus although Churchland thinks that he accepts a form of incommensurability, it is hard to see how he can, and certainly the form he offers is so weak as hardly to deserve the name.

The point is, I think, that Stich and Churchland are in the grip of a realist theory here. The temptation is to think of a layer of mental facts which are represented by our beliefs and then to imagine further that these facts could be represented in quite a different way, as an array of neurones and synapses, for example. What I argue is that beliefs are already like theory-encoded facts precisely because of their intensionality. So any rival theory must give us the same understanding of these as our present untutored 'folk psychological' theory. But this effectively excludes replacement. Either we have replaced it with something which is not the same belief, as in my Freudian example, or we replace it with something which is not a belief at all, an arrangement of neurones or an internalised VDU. Here the minimum continuity required for it to be proper to speak of improvement or replacement seems to be missing. After all, if you think, like Stich, that irrationality is inadequately explained in terms of folk psychology, then one can only say that it is not explained at all in our grand new computational or neurobiological theory because nothing remotely resembling the concept is going to appear.

So the finale of this second argument runs like this: actions incorporate beliefs in as much as they are required to individuate actions. But the identity conditions for beliefs so intimately incorporate content as to render implausible the replacement of 'mental concepts' by alternatives. Given that those philosophers most anxious to classify common sense talk of the mind as folk psychology are also keen on its replacement by neurological or computational theory this objection is very telling.

The third and most general of the objections I shall make is to do with the idea that human behaviour can be explained in such a general way. Theoretical explanation, it has to be remembered, is an activity with a history. Somebody formulates or some group of people formulate a theory in order to explain certain puzzling phenomena; the theory is then communicated to others and it may come to enjoy wide currency so that it becomes the accepted explanation of phenomena previously found problematic. If we think of folk psychology in this way then we speculate that at some point in our distant past one or more of our ancestors, seeing a neighbour hurl a woolly rhinoceros bone at the wall with a howl, suddenly thought to himself: 'By Jove, he's angry; he has certain attitudes, beliefs and wishes with respect to the situation which in conjunction cause that behaviour.' Now the idea that anybody should have formulated such an hypothesis in such a way is as implausible as Russell's derisive hypothesis about the origins of language, that a group of hitherto speechless elders met and decided to call a wolf a 'wolf'. On the absurdity of this Patricia Churchland and I agree. But what alternative is there? Explanatory theories do not arise *ex nihilo*. For folk psychology to be an explanatory theory it is necessary that somebody should have designed it that way. But who could think this?

When I use the words 'He is angry', I may do so because I see straight off that the man is angry. I do not infer this from his behaviour. I am not hypothesising an inner state to explain his behaviour. Indeed for such 'mental predicates' to get off the ground it is necessary that some should be transparent. In the same way I know that I am in my study and not seated on Concorde. It is the Wittgensteinian move which I think is the point here. Statements like 'He is angry' may or may not be explanations depending on context, for theorising can take place in whatever terms we choose. The idea that there is a fixed language of theorising involving a vocabulary of specifically theoretical terms, an idea which consumed so many man-hours a few decades ago, is so much eyewash; of course, in making a statement like 'He is angry' I have further commitments; I expect the man to act in certain ways and if he does not so react, then I will have second thoughts. What does seem wrong is to suggest that the original introduction of such terms was an explanatory move or that we postulate the existence of inner states. This arbitrarily invests ordinary talk about the mind with philosophical dualism. Churchland can easily allow that these terms can now be used straight off in as much as we have absorbed their theoretical function into our descriptive repertoire, but if their initial use was explanatory then it becomes unclear how we could have learnt or taught the relevant concepts in the first place. 'Anger' must already be given some sense in order to occur in an explanation and for this to be the case some concepts in this group must have been introduced in a descriptive mode.

Once this is accepted we have no need either of Wilkes's suggestion, that terms such as 'belief' or 'anger' be given an instrumental reading. They too can be attributed 'straight off' and when they are, they are not necessarily means to making predictions, means which carry no ontological weight. Remember that if we understand them as conservatives were enjoined to understand the Copernican system, as simply useful devices for making predictions, then we are open to the objection that they will then have no explanatory value at all. For the point about an instrumentalist interpretation is that explanatory value drops out. They are good for prediction and nothing else. Presumably Wilkes takes this view because she thinks that 'mental' terms do not refer; there are no such things as beliefs and emotions. But it is always open to her to follow the Churchlands in assuming folk psychology to be an explanatory theory of sorts, vitiated by the fact that the elements thought to exist do not exist in fact. For my own part, reference seems no big deal. I have no objection to saying that 'Beethoven's choral symphony' does not refer since there is nothing I can point to, certainly not the score or a performance. But I certainly wish to say that the choral symphony exists, just as I want to say that my irritation with eliminativist materialists exists. Wilkes's difficulty stems from the belief she shares with the Churchlands, that beliefs are 'inner states'.

Theorising is a form of explaining, often, though not invariably, a form where the explaining is less certain or confident. In order for theorising to take place, something must be explained or an attempt made at explaining it. This explanans might itself be a piece of theorising at some point or another but it does not have to be and it will not be at the point at which explanation takes place. In this way descriptions are prior to explanation. Now the fact that when we describe we bring what we describe under concepts should not be confused, as it often is, with the process of explanation. From the fact that there are no descriptions without concepts, it does not follow that every description is a sort of truncated explanation. To speak for the moment in vulgar Kantianism, to place a sensation under a concept is not *ipso facto* to record or to postulate an explanation. For explanations essentially involve relationships of dependence and such a relationship is not necessarily involved here. At the heart of the Churchlands' argument here may be an equivocation on 'theory'. For the move from the premise that every description involves concepts and is theoretical in that sense to the conclusion that all such descriptions are scientific explanations *manqué* is the crucial error.

Certainly an observation may be regarded as true whilst being couched in a theoretical vocabulary which is now *passé* because the theory is false, so there can be no objection in principle to the idea that our modes of describing the mind are replete with outmoded theory. It does not follow that everything we say commits us to any theory which the language incorporates. When I speak of seeing the sunrise, for example, I do not thereby commit myself to Ptolemaic theory. No doubt talk of sunrises invites some theoretical extrapolation and this may be true when we speak of human behaviour in terms which betray their metaphorical origin. If we describe somebody as defensive then certain moves towards a theory look more likely than others. But if all descriptions of the mind entailed an explanatory theory, the explanations would become tautological. The generalisations about human behaviour cited by the Churchlands may be trivial but they are not tautological. So there is an important distinction here between the idea that talk of the mind comes trailing bits of theory and the idea that talk of the mind is explanatory of behaviour. The first is true in the sense that the application of concepts invariably has implications which take us beyond the here and now. The second is only sometimes true, as I have shown.

These considerations do not suggest that folk psychology is not a possible theory. It is a way of explaining the complex and resourceful behaviour of *homo sapiens* which might occur to Martians. But its advocates do not claim that it is a possible theory but that it actually is a theory. For it to be an actual theory it is necessary that somebody offer it as such. Whatever it may be for Venusians, Martians or Professors Churchland or Stich (who after all may be evidence that we are not alone), it is not a possible theory for us.

There is a large and interesting class of ideas about human beings which reflects beliefs which are specific to a culture. States such as anomie, alienation, accidie and angst go with a whole galaxy of attitudes and theories about people which may percolate into the general consciousness. At one time, perhaps, the theory of humours had the status now accorded to talk about 'defensive reactions'. We speak so generally nowadays about complexes and about the unconscious that it is quite allowable to speak of such theories as part of the ordinary commerce of thought and discussion. If by folk psychology is meant such an eclectic *ad hoc* assemblage of bits of half digested Adler and Freud, then there is no harm in the idea and I would be the first to agree that common sense explanation of human behaviour is imbued with such theorising. The problem is that believers in folk psychology have wished to classify all our mental ascriptions as theory. The verdict is inescapable. This is utterly implausible.

4

AKRASIA AND SELF DECEPTION

'I did this,' said my memory. 'I cannot have done this,' said my pride and remains inexorable. In the end, memory yields.

Quoted to Freud by the 'Rat man'

I

What is the problem about akrasia? It is obvious, is it not, that sometimes we act unwisely and against our own interests and fail to do what we should. We are weak willed. A paradigm case is that of the man who ought not to drink because he is driving home and yet, liking a drink, succumbs to the temptation. We say that if his will were stronger, he would have acted differently.

I shall follow current philosophical usage in my use of 'akrasia'. It is more frequently translated by 'incontinence' than by 'weakness of will', though Davidson takes it to be aptly rendered by the latter.[1] The problems of finding an equivalent in English are highlighted by his uncertainty, for we do not think of somebody who cannot control his bowels as being weak willed, at least not normally. Judging from Aristotle's usage, 'weakness of will' is closer to 'akrasia' than 'incontinence'. Pears follows Liddell and Scott in recommending 'lack of self control'.[2]

The problem about akrasia is not dissimilar to the problem about self deception. The problem about self deception is that it invites construction on the model of lying. Self deception is then lying to oneself. But there is evidently something quite extraordinary about the notion of deceiver and deceived being the same person. If you are in the position of deceiver, you can hardly be deceived. You know what is going on because you are doing it. Equally, there is a tendency to suppose that it cannot be the case

74

that you do not want to do what you do as long as you act voluntarily. After all, if you are a free agent, what you do is at your own behest. You are the author of your acts and it can neither be the case that what you are doing is what you would rather not do, nor that you wish you were doing what you do not do. And yet we do not think that St Paul was guilty of some sort of logical error when he said: 'That which I would do, I do not and that which I would not, that I do.'

Now the reason why akrasia is so crucial to the problem which I have set myself is that akrasia invites a 'deep structure', 'essence' or 'hidden mechanism' model. Until recently, hardly any writer on the topic rejected the assumption of multiple agents within the person with consequent difficulties both in ontology and in the solution of the question of akrasia.[3] The crudest form of evasion of the problem, for example, follows Freud in distinguishing separate agents within the person each with their own motivations and degrees of awareness. But this immediately brings us up against further difficulties. Neither akrasia nor self deception can occur unless the same individual is the subject of whatever is going on. The deception is a deceiving of oneself. Akrasia is a failure to do what one recognises is the best. Not much is to be gained from replicating the logical problems of the doctrine of the Trinity.

However if we, alternatively, stress the unity of the agent, we bring about the collapse of akrasia into something else in a different way. First of all we may think of the agent as being overwhelmed by his desires so that he simply always does what he desires. This is the ever present threat for a philosopher who construes desires as causes, taking action to be determined by the preponderance of causal factors. The agent desires to have the drink and also not to drive home under the influence. The desire to have the drink simply outweighs the desire not to. But the internal unity of the person is bought at a price and the price is that akrasia disappears. It is now no more than one form of conflict between desires in which the strongest desire triumphs. It is hard to square this with freedom, for we imagine that a man exercises his freedom at least partly in not doing what he desires. A person is not like an animal. He can desire something but opt not to pursue it.

Parenthetically, I do not believe that conflict between desires is all that common. There are occasions, of course. The sweet trolley after dinner is, for me, the paradigm of conflict between desires. But one indication of the way in which the concept of desire is being moved from its ordinary habitat is the way in which conflicts between desires are multiplied by this theory.

The second way in which akrasia may be extinguished has a variant. If we take desires to be reasons for action and take the totality of desires as the totality of reasons, then we can conclude that the agent both has a reason for taking the drink and a reason for not taking it. In such a case the decision to have the drink represents the way the reasons fall; it is the way the weighting turns out. Providing no miscalculation has taken place, the decision to have the drink is not irrational after all on this basis. Now such a conclusion denies one of the main characteristics of akrasia, and that is that the akrates is irrational. For an irrational act is taken as being against the reasons and the taking of the drink cannot be said to be against the reasons if the reasons in totality favour it.

The especially problematic form which akrasia takes for Davidson derives from his regarding desires as reasons in precisely this way for he thinks of desires as reasons for action.[4] It then becomes incumbent upon him to find a way in which akrasia can occur given these assumptions. What he maintains is that the action which is akratic is, all things considered, not the best but that, relativised to what the agent desires at one point, it is grounded in those desires. But this turns akrasia into what it is not, a species of intellectual failure, for the agent has failed to take into consideration all the relevant factors. It comes close to the Aristotelian conception of akrasia as a form of forgetting. In this case some of the factors which are pertinent to the decision simply have not been taken into account.

It is, in any case, a fundamental error to suppose that to have a desire for x is necessarily to have a reason for securing x. It may not be. To have a reason for x-ing or for securing x requires that x either be seen as worthy in itself or as a means to a worthy end. Neither is necessarily fulfilled if I just desire x.

The traditional rejoinder at this point is to argue that getting what you desire gives pleasure and that the pleasure is the good that confers reason status. In considering this, first of all let us get one howler out of the way. Desires are not propositions and reasons are; so reasons and desires cannot be identical. However, desires do have an intensional content, and the question now becomes whether having a desire for x or a desire to do x entails having a reason for securing x or for doing x. Certainly, you may argue to yourself that if you satisfy your desire you will get pleasure and that since the pleasure is good you have a reason to secure x or to do x. But it is bad philosophical psychology to claim that this is universally the case. As Bradley pointed out at length, our actions are not usually or even often motivated by the belief that pleasure will follow. Of course, once ratiocination about pleasure enters the picture, we have the possibility of a conflict of reasons. Suppose the balance of the reasons favours not doing x but still I do x, do we have akrasia? The answer is that if the agent draws the wrong conclusion from the balance of reasons then we have intellectual failure. If that intellectual failure is itself motivated then we have, as I shall argue, something rather like a further form of akrasia. If not, that is if I do x because I desire to and take no notice of the results of the ratiocination, then we have the commoner form of akrasia. In this case the reasoning is no more than conceptual icing on a volitional cake. The point upon which I want to insist is that characteristically when I do x I do it because I want to and that the reason why I want to is not because I reflect upon the pleasure I will get. I may want to do something for its own sake or I may want something because it is a means to another end I value but it is quite rare for that other end to be pleasure. In any case, as we have seen, some actions are done on whim. Although desire mediated through reflection on pleasure does occur, I think it is pretty uncommon. Furthermore the pleasure itself may not be good; the pleasures of gloating or of sadism, for example, cannot count as reasons for action unless the agent's value system is also perverted. But the case has been, I think, sufficiently made out without our needing to consider such exceptional circumstances.

Even more generally one cannot validly infer that if somebody wants x then he or she has a reason for getting x nor if he or she has a reason to secure x, he or she necessarily wants x. Human beings are not like this. Indeed, a major flaw in Davidson's analysis of akrasia is that in his principle P2 he subscribes to the thesis that if A has a reason to do x then he wants to do x (I take it that 'it would be better to do x' entails that he has a reason to do x).[5] The principle reads as follows: 'If an agent judges that it would be better to do x than to do y then he wants to do x more than he wants to do y.' I assume that the non-comparative form would also be acceptable to Davidson. Conversely there are indications that Davidson believes that the converse holds and that to have a desire is to have a reason. Following Aristotle he describes the desire to know the time as being conceived as a principle of action whose natural propositional expression would be something like: 'It would be good for me to know the time.'[6]

There is a third way in which akrasia may disappear. The agent may revalue his position; he looks at the situation and decides that there are no strong reasons against taking the drink. The difference is that here we no longer think of the agent as simply the plaything of his desires and his action as determined by the preponderance of factors bearing upon him. Rather we think of him as actively weighing the pros and cons. He is an agent. Davidson prefers this view of the will as a *tertium quid*. However, it runs into difficulties in inviting that type of ontology which sees the agent as battling against impulses from his animal nature, an implicit ontology which is the main target of this book. I maintain that the problems of akrasia and self deception can be met without multiplying entities within the agent.

The Socratic problem about akrasia depends upon akrasia collapsing into one or other of the two last forms. In both cases we do what seems to be good, in the first case because the reasons turn out that way (desires counting as reasons), and in the second because we have revalued. The puzzle was then how akrasia could occur at all. How could a man see the good and not desire it?

It has been claimed that the revaluation could be intellectual failure. Either I am mistaken about the goodness of taking the drink, or in the derivation of the conclusion of the practical syllogism there occurs some fairly gross error. In either case it is simply an error in ratiocination and nothing more. I want to suggest that there are fairly strong grounds for doubting whether I can innocently mistake the grounds for my action in this way. We are asked to believe that my judgement that I can take the extra drink could be just a mistake; I somehow miscalculate the forces of the grounds against having that extra glass. But is this plausible? Most of us would, I think, be inclined to conclude that anybody who reasoned thus was self deceiving. To be generous to the drinker requires opening a gap between the conditions for self deception and the criteria by which we judge that an agent is self deceived. Such a gap between criteria and conditions requires that it be possible that the agent is really not self deceived when the behavioural criteria for self deception are satisfied. The facts and the evidence split; reality and appearance diverge. Now, I am not persuaded that the kind of realist position advocated by Pears, for one, with respect to these mental facts is possible. It could be, I think, that the evidence is not sufficient for us to conclude that the drinker is self deceiving. He might only have had one glass, for example, and, on non-party nights, he is not that vehement in his denunciation of drinking and driving. In such cases we could say that he might be self deceiving without the evidence amounting to conclusive proof. I would rather choose to say that there is no answer to this question. But suppose that he is normally highly critical of people who drink and drive, he has had some drinks, though nothing like enough to cause him to be in a muddled state of mind, and he argues that he would be quite safe taking another glass. Imagine that, in the terms of the earlier argument, a revaluation has taken place. Could such a revaluation be innocent? For this to be the case it must be that the indications of self deception do not correspond to the facts. Let us try to conceive a case. It might be that he is 'saying in his heart' that the reasons are that he only takes this drink to mislead the onlookers into thinking that he is weak willed. We could think that he thinks it is in his long term interests to give an impression that he is not fully in control. Perhaps he is about to clinch an important business deal. Does this private performance constitute an internal fact about him with which the behavioural criteria clash?

The problem is, of course, whether we (or he) should take what he says in his heart at face value (if this is not too paradoxical a way of speaking). He can, of course, simply compound the self deception by telling himself a story and once again the check on the truth of that story comes from how it meshes with grosser behavioural features. If he tells us his private thought we could judge that he is self deceived and we judge in the usual way. We watch the alacrity with which he rushes to the bar etc. What I suggest, then, is that no essentialist account could countermand our judgement of self deception. There is no level of facts which could be such as to cancel that. If there were a true essentialist account, to know it would be to eradicate the self deception, but there is no such account.

Now akrasia, typically, though not necessarily, occurs where a long term commitment clashes with a short term desire. The agent in my example wants to have the drink but he also wants to be a responsible human being and not somebody who has run down some innocent bystander under the influence of drink. 'Want' cannot be replaced by 'desire' with perfect propriety here. For he does not desire to be responsible. 'Desire' is appropriate for wanting food, sex or material gew-gaws, etc. The celibate may have desires which he does not want to gratify. We can say quite properly that our drinker has a reason for not driving home, whereas we cannot say that he has a reason for taking the drink (namely that he wants to). As we have seen, he might not want to accede to the desire. We say this because I have a reason to do x if x is either good in itself or a means to a good. So a clash between reason and desire is possible; I may have a reason not to do x because it is bad in itself or because it has or may have bad consequences, and yet I may desire x. Thus though I desire to have the drink, if I am strong willed I will not take the drink, assuming the reason or reasons against it are not known to me.[7]

We think of reasons, particularly prudential reasons, as applying over a period of time. It is natural to think of desires as relatively short lived and reasons as essentially long term. So it is worth pointing out that I can sometimes forget the reason I have for abstaining from x whilst the desire to do x remains as strong as ever; the reason still applies, of course, but it is no longer part of my ratiocinative stock, so to speak. Equally, my desire to improve my piano playing can be a long term desire, staying with me throughout my life, whilst the reason I have to offer first aid to the accident victim only exists as long as he needs help.

These cases are, however, not the common run. As Kenny observes,[8] general commitments show themselves over a lifetime and we could always make a case for subsuming my reason for helping the accident victim under a general prescription that we should help fellow humans in need, though I am not convinced that this answers to the situational character of everyday moral experience. Although the primitive sign of a want may be trying to get,[9] nevertheless this cannot be translated into a simplistic rule that unless you try to get x whenever possible you do not want x. It is precisely this simplistic version that creates problems for Davidson's type of analysis.

A man is not regarded as prudent if his long term plans are evil. We do not call the miser or the brains behind the Great Train Robbery prudent. The prudent man has a wide range of desires and motives. Prudence is a virtue possessed by integrated persons. Mabbutt, to whom this account is indebted, describes him as 'balanced'.[10] The prudent man may foresee that a certain desire will arise and make provision to satisfy it or to forestall it. As

Mabbutt recognises, the existence of such second order motives renders the Humean picture of man as the forum of competing desires wholly implausible.

The next point to which I want to draw attention is that only some sorts of reasons count in an akratic conflict. Dorothy Walsh distinguishes two forms of akrasia, moral transgression and prudential folly.[11] Commonly, however, the examples given are of the latter. The man who takes the extra drink acts wrongly, certainly, but it is not because of that we regard him as weak willed; he is weak willed because he is imprudent and knowingly imprudent. You risk misery and the loss of much which you value if you drink and drive. Or take the case where, despite your commitment to a low chloresterol diet, you succumb to temptation and take an extra slice. The reasons which conflict with desire in weakness of will are prudential.

Now it might appear that prudence cannot be quite the talisman we seek. Mele, who is very fertile in producing counter-examples, produces the case of a boy who tries to break into a house for a dare but whose nerve fails him at the last moment. Is this weakness of will? It certainly seems like it. However, it does not seem right to describe it as imprudent. A prudent action would have been not to try to break in in the first place. It seems that one could be weak willed in failing to carry through a course which one was imprudent in commencing, and it looks like a counter-example to the general thesis that akratic actions are imprudent.

I think this can be handled. The Davidsonian switch from an 'all things considered' point of view to a more limited perspective is relevant here though it does not help with the more general question of akrasia. The boy who thinks he 'ought' to break in but fails is, from his limited point of view, imprudent. He loses face and loses position amongst his peers. From the general position the boy's action is unquestionably imprudent but he does not see this. A misjudgement is central here. Even if the dare is self inflicted and there is no peer group pressure it will still be the case that he may argue with himself in favour of the long term advantages of sticking to his guns and getting into the habit of seeing through enterprises.

Of all the great philosophers of the past, Joseph Butler might seem to have possessed the moral psychology requisite to handle akrasia. However, Butlerian prudence, 'cool or reasonable self love' as he called it, embraces moral virtue so that moral weakness is a form of imprudence. He thus conflates what I take to be two separate cases, moral weakness and akrasia.

For a moral conflict where desire wins over duty does not count as weakness of will even though prudential elements may be present where the motivation is complex. I ought to visit a bereaved friend but Manchester United are playing Liverpool on television and I succumb to the temptation to stay at home and watch the match. I act selfishly but I do not display weakness of will.

This conclusion is reinforced by two arguments. First, all weakness of will is irrational. But it is not contrary to rationality as currently conceived to neglect duty for desire and hence it is not weakness of will. Second, consider the scope of akrasia. Prudential considerations are concerned with my own future, of course. But I can act akratically with respect, and only with respect, to those individuals whose interests I identify with my own. If my small child asks me for sweets, I might indulgently give him sweets. Indulgence is like self indulgence and self indulgence is often a fairly central form of akrasia; only in such cases as a deliberated decision to give oneself a holiday from demanding standards would it not be akratic. So I may know that I have a reason not to give the child sweets. It is imprudent because it is bad for his teeth. We can extend this to any individual to whom I am, metaphorically or actually, *in loco parentis*. To give somebody else's children sweets may be akratic, though it is moral weakness and not akrasia to encourage imprudence in an autonomous adult. The point is beautifully made by Aristotle. 'Parents love their children as themselves, for having been split off from them they are, as it were, other selves, selves at a distance.'[12] (Though it would be a mistake to suppose that one's love for one's children was explained in any way by being shown to be a form of self love. That is certainly not so. One's love for one's children does not need any explanation and that is why it can be called 'natural'.) So prudence and interest intermesh in the way my thesis predicts. For weakness of will to be a form of moral weakness it is necessary to have duties to oneself.

Parenthetically, the agent's estimate of his own interests is what matters here. A man does not cease to be imprudent because what he thought was counter to his interests, the satisfaction of a particular desire (which he goes ahead and satisfies), turns out not to be. So we answer in the negative to Aristotle's question as to whether the continent man abides by the right choice. A strong willed man is a man who forms intentions on the basis of reasons and carries them out. In part this is a matter of selective attention. He pays attention to his reasons rather than to his desires. Think what we say to a man who is overcome by a desire. We tell him to think of the consequences. 'If you drive in that condition you could kill somebody. At the least you might injure yourself, cause hundreds of pounds of damage to your car and lose your licence.' We try to make him form intentions on the basis of reasons. We cannot produce such an account of akrasia by taking it simply to be a conflict of desires. For in a conflict of desires no moral obloquy is necessarily attached to one choice or the other.

II

How, then, does self deception fit into all this? The paradoxical feature of self deception is that the self deceiver seems both to know the information which he suppresses, for otherwise how can he suppress it, and at the same time, through the act of suppressing, not know it. This aspect of self deception is treated by Demos on the analogy of lying.[13] Demos chooses to regard self deception as lying to oneself. The conclusion he draws is that the deceiver, failing to attend to his beliefs, overlooks or fails to notice one of his beliefs and is thus inconsistent (which rather falls short of lying). But inconsistency is common and is not necessarily self deception; the important point is that the self deceiver purposefully ignores one of his beliefs. The model of lying suggests a systemic approach. Pears has recently argued that the model requires that one of the competing agents be informed about the other in an asymmetrical way. Rather curiously he adds that the split between agents may be temporary and last only as long as the campaign, so to speak, and, on this, Davidson concurs. But this brings the matter perilously close to the temporary possession of desires, reasons or motives and the ignorance of the party of at least some of them. Put this way, it seems that we can equally well explain the matter in hand in terms of the common sense ontology of conflicting desires and motives; then the move to sub-agency does look both otiose and metaphysically extravagant.[14]

Although lying is a helpful analogy, it fails in as much as the self deceiver is, to a large degree, unaware that he is lying to himself. Though he has an inkling that his behaviour can be seen in another and less favourable light, he does not set out to deceive himself with quite the element of conscious purposefulness that the model of lying implies for otherwise he would be fully aware that he is lying and, although deceiving, he would not himself be deceived. And here is the nub, the puzzle involved in self deception. For it is necessary to be, to an extent, purposeful in the deception; otherwise it is not deception but merely inconsistency or falsehood; yet it cannot be so conscious a purpose for then the deception fails simply because the individual knows what is going on.

I have spoken of an inkling. What is this inkling? Clearly there are occasions where a person may conceal something from himself without it counting as self deception. There is a fine classification here which writers have not always spotted. We can imagine somebody of whom we might wish to say that he really acted from selfish motives whilst thinking he acted from altruistic ones. Yet we may not necessarily be justified in concluding that he deceives himself. For like many people, his capacity for self criticism may be underdeveloped. Without the capacity to see oneself in an unfavourable light, self deception is an impossibility; but the possibility of self criticism is not enough. It is also necesary that there be an inkling as to one's real motives, motives which may become apparent in such giveaways as Freudian slips in conversation or behaviour. The way this 'inkling' operates is roughly as follows.

A person becomes aware that there is a description of his act in terms of other motives; although aware of its existence, he chooses not to explore this by formulating a detailed description and assessing whether or not it accurately describes his behaviour. The inkling is an uneasy feeling, a suspicion not made clear to oneself. Thus the refusal to pursue self examination to the point where he might uncover discrepancies between behaviour and principles reveals the degree to which he suppresses the inkling. If he clearly formulates the disturbing description and refuses to accept it because it is unwelcome he might be self deceiving to the extent that he had an inkling that he was committing the fallacy of special pleading. At any level of analysis or self criticism, self deception may arise. He may suppress a sense of the incompatibility between the two explicitly formulated descriptions of his behaviour, thus producing yet a third alternative. To revert to the earlier formulations, the agent does not pursue the evidence; he does not press enquiries. He does not want to disturb.

Like the akrates, the irrationality of the self deceiver lies in his action. His desire that the facts should be one way rather than another clashes with his long term commitment, shared by all of us, that his beliefs should accord with the facts. He does not want it to be the case that his son is a receiver of stolen goods and turns away from the evidence which suggests that conclusion. In general he recognises, with the rest of us, that it is a good thing that his beliefs be true beliefs; in the particular case this requires that he face the evidence squarely and see where it leads. This he fails to do and his failure is a weakness of will. But note that it is weakness of will rather than akrasia. Classical accounts of the akrates show him as losing self control or succumbing to the weight of passions or desires or being unable to resist an urge.

The important thing here is that the weakness shows itself in the action. The weak willed man fails to investigate where he should. It is not like wishful thinking where there is just no evidence to support the wished for conclusion. Nor is it intellectual sloth which Charlton mentions in his very wide ranging and scholarly analysis of types of weakness of will. In the case of self deception the evidence actually runs counter to the beliefs and, typically, the self deceiver does not pursue the evidence. In some respects, as we have seen, this is quite unlike the standard cases of akrasia or even the usual cases of weakness of will. We do not often have a passion or urge not to investigate which overwhelms the prudent desire to find out how the facts lie. The likely cases are indeed quite the opposite. We could think of a person as possessed by curiosity which he is unable to restrain. That might be akratic. But omissions will not generally be so. We could imagine that a man cannot bring himself to look into a sink of iniquity. He cannot bring himself to learn about the British occupation of Tasmania in the last century, for instance. But these are certainly unusual cases.

Obviously there are cases where the evidence forces itself upon my attention and where I have no option but to believe what I believe. There might seem to be a parallel in those cases where it is perfectly obvious what I ought to do if I am to obtain some particular end. But there are differences. I can always choose not to do something whilst it is in my power, whereas I cannot refrain from believing that there is a keyboard in front of me. It is for this reason that I choose to speak of the weak willed self deceiver as displaying his weakness in the gathering of evidence. It is what he fails to do rather than what he fails to believe that shows self deception.

What is prudential is the general policy that we investigate the evidence relevant to our beliefs. The self deceiver ducks this on specific occasions when he suspects that the evidence may not turn out to his liking. It clashes with a general commitment to making one's beliefs true.

A.R. Mele, in an interesting recent contribution,[15] does make the connection between akrasia and self deception but, I think, not always in the right sort of way. First, he argues that the self deceiver is typically motivated by a desire to believe that p without intending deception. Strictly, however, the self deceiver does not want to believe that p. He wants that p be the case; there is a considerable and obvious difference. Mele believes that the self-deceiver does not intend to deceive himself; self deception involves intention but in a different way. He lists four ways in which self deception may occur.

1 Negative misinterpretation, where the evidence is wrongly construed as not counting against p, p being the proposition he wishes were true.
2 Positive misinterpretation where the evidence is taken to be favourable when it is really unfavourable.
3 Selective focusing where the agent pays more attention to evidence favouring p than the evidence which runs counter to p.
4 Selective evidence gathering.

The intentional behaviour involved relates to the collection and assessment of evidence. The essential point on which Mele and I agree is that agency is central to self deception. We agree, too, on rejecting multiple personality explanations.

What this leaves obscure is, of course, why we should speak of 'self deception' here. The way I have presented the matter centres on the fact that the agent's suspicions lead him to avoid pressing the matter. The man is not inconsistent. He does not believe both that his son is and is not guilty of receiving. He believes that his son is innocent but is troubled by the possibility of his guilt and by the likelihood, though not certainty, that if he were to make further enquiries or consider further the evidence he would find out that his son was breaking the law. This is certainly a paradigm case of self deception and I think it follows that there is something curious and rather misleading about the term. The facts are not quite precisely caught by the term 'self deception' which, when taken literally, does entail some inconsistency. It is not a well chosen phrase but we are presumably stuck with it. We can imagine that, confronted with the evidence, he might still refuse to believe it, spinning some complicated story which explains his son's behaviour. Whether this is plain inconsistency, a sort of double-think, is not obvious and the boundaries may be imprecise here. (It is interesting to note that Orwell's term has caught on; perhaps there was a gap in the conceptual net which needed filling and Orwell's neologism does the job.)

In two recent papers, 'How easy is akrasia?' and 'Motivated irrationality', [16] David Pears discusses the relation of self deception to akrasia. These are, I think, the most interesting contributions to the topic to appear since classical times. Pears subdivides self deception. We can deceive ourselves either through a faulty assessment of evidence or by a failure to monitor our feelings and motives. Rather characteristically he fails to give examples, but presumably a case of the first might be our example of the man who refuses to concede that his son is a receiver despite the evidence, whilst an example of the second might be our drinker's assessment of his motive for having the extra drink as being his wish not to be discourteous to his host. The 'latitude', as Pears calls it, between evidence and conclusion which the self deceiver exploits can appear in various ways. I may persuade myself that the reason against my belief may be countered by reasons in favour of it which happen not to be available as yet, or that the reasons in favour may, again unbeknown to me at present, be wrong. Third, I might simply miscalculate the relative force of the reasons. Only the first two count as self deception and, once again, the difference between plain inconsistency and self deception shows in whether the self deceiver hesitates about pressing his investigations to the usual limit. If he holds off then we have self deception. But if all the facts are in and he believes in the teeth of the evidence, then we are close to inconsistency, depending on whether he tries to open a gap between the evidence and the conclusion the evidence clearly recommends. If he tries to open a gap then we have self deception. If he acknowledges that there is no gap then we have inconsistency. The closing of the gap may be either a matter of inference or a matter of empirical research.

Pears gives one over-riding reason as to why akrasia in action is easier than self deception. It is that desires are more appropriate causes of action than beliefs. It is hard to gauge the force of this argument. We feel that it ought to show that desires cannot cause beliefs at all rather than that its causal force is somehow mitigated. It could be read as suggesting that akrasia in belief is more irrational than akrasia in action, perhaps because it is closer to self contradiction. The problem with self deception is so to present it that it is not equivalent to self contradiction. This can, I think, be done, as I have tried to show here, but in order to do it we need to show that self deception is closer to akrasia than Pears imagines. As I have indicated, I believe that standard weakness of will is the only element in self deception at all close to akrasia.

Davidson's classic presentation of the problem of akrasia involves two principles:[17]

P1 If an agent wants to do x more than he wants to do y and believes himself free to do either x or y then he will intentionally do x if he does either x or y intentionally.

P2 If an agent judges that it would be better to do x than to do y, then he wants to do x more than he wants to do y.

P3 There are incontinent actions.

P1, P2 and P3 form an inconsistent triad.

Let us allow that in deciding whether to believe p or not we need to find out whether or not p is true. So a parallel to Davidson's P1 and P2 will read:

P1' If an agent wants to find out whether p is true more than he wants not to find out and he believes himself free either to find out or not to find out, then he will intentionally find out if he either finds out or does not find out intentionally (assuming the truth of p is discoverable).

P2' If an agent judges that it would be better to find out what the case is than not, then he wants to find out if p holds more than he wants not to find out.

Now obviously P2' is as weak as P2. From the fact that I judge it better to find out it does not follow that I want to find out. The self deceiver, I propose, is precisely in this position. He judges it better, as a matter of general prudence, that his beliefs match the facts. Just as it is imprudent to drive under the influence since I risk getting caught, even though the chances may not be high, so it is imprudent not to match belief and fact even though the consequences of not doing so might not be particularly damaging in this case. But to match beliefs and fact requires finding out what the evidence is, and this is a matter of action. Characteristically the self deceiver has an inkling that the evidence might prove damaging to cherished beliefs, and he does not pursue it. The irrationality of this is not the stark irrationality of self contradiction but the irrationality of weakness of will, which is in turn the irrationality of imprudence. Indeed, without the stress on imprudence, it is hard to see what is wrong with self deception. It is not obviously immoral.

Pears's book, *Motivated Irrationality*,[18] sees him moving away from a sharp contrast between akrasia and self deception. At several points he suggests that self deception is a form of akrasia, and acknowledges the importance of prudence. This raises a problem which applies equally to my account. It may not be conspicuously imprudent to fail to believe what the evidence points towards. Now akratic behaviour is imprudent behaviour; the satisfying of a passing whim or even of a deeper desire runs counter to the agent's longer term interests. But although we can certainly make out a case for claiming that as a general rule it is in an agent's interests that his beliefs accord with the facts, it may not be so in particular cases. Thus, it may well be prudent for me to continue to believe that my brother-in-law is an honourable man rather than to face the consequences of knowing that he is a cad and a bounder. Life may be less stressful lived in ignorance. Equally, on one particular occasion my drinking myself insensate caused me to miss the bus which crashed on the motorway with the loss of all hands. In both cases there may be particular occasions when akrasia has beneficial results, although in general akrasia runs counter to prudential behaviour. Likewise with self deception. It may be more comfortable to be self deceived, though this may not always be so; as Davidson points out, the self deceiver may actually make his life a misery. Imagine a man driven by jealousy who sees constant evidence of infidelity where none exists. Still, the general principle seems to hold; in advance of the sort of knowledge of particular cases which would, in any case, dissolve the self deception, it is prudent to try to match belief and the world.

However, at least part of the question remains unanswered. Is there not something strange about calling self deception imprudent? This may be. But there is nothing strange about calling a failure to investigate imprudent, and it is just there that the nub of deception is to be found.

Pears accounts for the various forms of irrationality in terms of what may be called a 'systemic approach' whereby we may see irrationality as a case where part of the personality acts against the main part. The major objection to this must be that it threatens the unity of the personality and, by doing so, turns self deception and akrasia into cases of conflict against persons or quasi persons which are sub-agents within the personality. Pears recognises that his arguments lead in this direction and is, in consequence, prepared to relax the conditions of identity even to the point of characterising the main system and the sub-system in different ways. For example he describes the main system as egoistic and the sub-system as altruistic.[19] However, the destructive force of this apparently escapes him. We have now collapsed akrasia into something different, namely conflict. To avoid this we must insist that the sub-systems of the person be identified as states of the person. But if that is conceded then the introduction of 'system' becomes just a verbal manoeuvre. The system theory is either too strong or too weak. If it is reducible to talk of the states of the person it is too weak. If the sub-systems have independence it seems too strong.

Second, there is a suspicion of the *ad hoc* about the introduction of system theory. This Pears is aware of. The alternative, however, is what he terms 'attribution theory' and he rejects attribution theory as rationalising and simplifying.[20] On this theory the attribution of beliefs to the agent is as much and no more than is required to explain the phenomena which puzzle. So we invest the person with just as much as is required to explain the behaviour but do not theorise further. What may be at the back of Pears's mind here is the thought that the attributionist is akin to the instrumentalist in physical science who denies the existence of sub-observational mechanisms to account for phenomena at the fringe of visibility. The difference between this and the microphysical original will surely be that further instrument assisted observation confirms the hypotheses of the microphysicist whereas no such observations will be forthcoming in the case of a systems account of mental life. Indeed there is a simple reason why instrumentalism is not appropriate here. We explain behaviour when we point to akrasia and self deception. But instrumentalist theories predict rather than explain.

A.R. Mele argues, to my mind very convincingly, that there are various ways in which akrasia can be explained without recourse to the sub-division of personality. Sometimes the incontinent action offers more immediate rewards than does a more prudent course. A one night stand might seem more fun; sometimes the agent just is not motivated strongly enough in favour of the long term considerations; like Amelie Rorty's, Mele's account has the great strength of connecting with our common sense explanations of how and why people fail. For what he describes are without doubt the ways that an agent will explain his akrasia (without necessarily excusing it). Rorty points out that habit often undermines good intentions. The habitual smoker is more likely to be akratic. Equally what is socially encouraged may be hard to resist. The third of Mele's four forms of explanation of akrasia is where the agent fails to use an effective process of self control. I might resist temptation by paying careful attention to the dangers of AIDS before contemplating a one night stand.

The important point is that these are all forms of explanation which do not require sub-agency and which form our ordinary patterns of the explanation of akrasia. For precisely this reason they explain akrasia whereas sub-agency does not.

Pears is committed to a form of that essentialism or realism which has been a principal target in this book. The realism appears early in the book. In the opening chapters he contrasts an inferential account of the features in which he is interested with an attributional theory. Like Freud, Pears seeks to extend hidden mechanism explanations from the natural sciences to the human sciences and it is my thesis that such an extension is not possible. What I am attempting is an account of weakness of will and self deception without recourse to hidden sub-systems and concealed mechanisms. In the next chapter I shall defend a hermeneutic and thematic analysis of mind. Before I do so I shall set the scene by contrasting two cases. Two men carry on working late into the night regularly and against doctor's orders. One does so because he is a workaholic who simply must go on working. 'Must' does not represent compulsion. The man is weak willed. He ought to stop and cannot. He wants to, of course. The second man goes on working because he thinks his work more important than his health. If he has to die he wants to die with his boots on. For realists like Pears and Freud, the difference is a difference between two different factual bases. There is a difference of fact between the first and the second and the difference lies in a belief which the second man has which the first does not share as well as in a difference of fact in the way the action is brought about by differing motives. (Assuming that differences of belief are differences in matters of fact; not all philosophers will agree.)

But there is also a moral difference. If we feel admiration for the first man it is a qualified admiration. Our admiration for the second is less qualified. Both act the same way. It would be untrue to say that the weak willed man could not do otherwise; this is a case of akrasia not compulsion. The counterfactuals are the same. What difference there is lies in the moral beliefs of the agent and that is a difference of fact between the two cases, of course. But that judgement reflects the agent's selective emphasis on one aspect of his life and does differentiate the two cases. One agent thinks that his work is of crucial importance to his life and that judgement determines our assessment of his act and character. We think that he, nobly though perhaps imprudently, judges that he does right to drive himself. The other does not place such a value on his desire to keep working. Central, then, in our estimate of the cases is this interpretative judgement about the moral element and such a feature resists a simplistic realism. It is often very difficult to separate matters of moral assessment from matters of fact about the mind.

Finally, how do we assess the two cases? We do so, not by the sort of enquiry which establishes the existence of sub-agents but by thematic analysis. When we discussed the case of the akratic drinker, the matter of his self deception was settled by looking at his reactions in relevant circumstances over a period of time. We will do the same in this case.

5

ON NOT TAKING THINGS AT FACE VALUE

What I have argued in this book is that what some philosophers have called a systemic approach to the mind is mistaken. It is wrong to think of the mind as though it is a structure which contains sub-agents which jointly create the macroscopic behaviour. Indeed, as I suggested in the last chapter but one, the very setting up of the problem in this way invites a dualism which provokes more problems than it solves.

However, I do not wish to deny the operation of desires and attitudes at different levels. As we have seen, we may want to have or not to have a desire. We can have attitudes to attitudes, attitudes towards desires and desires directed at desires. Animals and infants do, of course, value things. We can say of a cat that it likes some food better than others. What it cannot do, and remain an animal, is place a value on that preference. It cannot think that its liking for fish is a good thing because fish is nutritious or that a craving for chocolate is a regrettable bourgeois extravagance. It is, arguably, the possibility of these considerations of value, consistency and prudence, and the domination of one preference over another which make our conception of mind the conception of the mind of a person. After all, it is precisely the absence of higher level considerations which makes us think of animals as non-persons. Moreover it is moot as to whether it is appropriate to speak of minds unless these second level considerations are there. Of course, they are not always operative. I may react with anger as an animal is angry. Certainly I was angry because I thought I was kicked but there may be cases where I am, say, irritated by a fly without being aware that I am irritated and without therefore having particular beliefs about the situation which mediate my irritation. These must be close to what Wittgenstein calls 'natural' or 'primitive' reactions and the clue to understanding this important but obscure concept may be what unites us to the animals. Reflect on the fact that it seems proper to speak of a cat as conscious but not as having a mind. Yet cats certainly may show empathy with a distressed human being. To say these reactions are preconceptual is not simply to say that they are unaccompanied by belief but rather that the belief is not necessarily active in producing the appropriate response. The roots of our mental life lie in such reactions. They are the backdrop to my opening fable and they provide the most unrevisable of texts on which we exercise our interpretative procedure.

Perhaps it is worth adding a general rider. I am going to speak of human identity but the sense of human identity in which I am interested is different from that which seems to lie behind the discussions of personal identity amongst analytic philosophers.[1] My conception is dynamic. It is perhaps Hegelian rather than Kantian. On this conception a man's identity changes as his deepest beliefs change. But this is not the sense of identity involved when I speculate on why it is impossible that I might change into Mr Gorbachev. In my sense identity grows through my own self conception and through other people's conception of me. Some of these self conceptions will, as we have seen, involve self deception. So it is at this point that we need to return to the topics of akrasia and self deception. We need an analysis of both which will be narrative rather than systemic in form. One principal contention in this study is that akrasia, its broader kin, weakness of will, and self deception are not only characteristic of persons but tell us more about our nature than almost any other features.

My claim is that self deception can be understood without the need for interlocking systems of sub-persons mutually ignorant of the other's motives and purposes. The account I have given, in which the idea of an 'inkling' does the work, is consistent with the idea of a description of mental life as a single level narrative in which any distinction between deep and surface traits can be explained in terms of a thematic understanding of the personality, and in which a paratactic reorganisation of the elements of the narrative points to a certain interpretation of the narrative. Akratic behaviour can be given a similarly non-systematic account which makes no reference to underlying structure. All that is required is the contrast between different beliefs and desires. On the one hand we have the desire to do x and on the other the higher level belief that to satisfy desires of this sort is not a good thing. We need too the connected contrast between long term prudential wishes and short term desires. So higher and lower are not to be interpreted literally but rather in terms of the role they play in thematic interpretation. Generally speaking, it is 'higher level' or second order desires which are educed in a thematic understanding of a person's akratic behaviour because they appear at salient points where their presence is required to explain why an agent does not do what he apparently wants to do. Think of somebody who, if he is to do anything about some particular desire, has to knuckle down to second order considerations. Paradoxically, and the locution reveals the negligent way in which these metaphors were introduced, 'deep' interpretation here reveals 'higher level' desires. Note also that whether or not we are conscious of these desires is irrelevant. Nobody can deny that I may conceal my motives by keeping them to myself. Equally somebody else could find things out about me which I do not harbour as secret thoughts. My anger could be concealed in my actions, coming to light in something I do without it ever being the case that I think to myself at any time that my motives are one way or another.

The emphasis I have placed on the similarity between our encounter with art and our encounter with persons, the emphasis on selection and on paratactic, invites one obvious objection, an objection which uses one feature of our mental life which was significant in the discussion of the hypothesis of a folk psychology. It is that many of our ascriptions of mental predicates are made 'straight off'. There is nothing interpretative, selective or temporal in character about recognising that a man is angry except in rather special circumstances; the context and what we see enables us to say this directly.

This is so, of course, but it is not the whole story. The attribution we make is contingent on a number of factors, one of which is the absence of any reasons not to take this at face value. Human beings are unique in the virtuosity with which they can dissemble. The anger could have been deliberately fostered for effect. To set this possibility aside we need to know something of both context and character. To reverse the example for a minute, the way we recognise dissembling is by seeing the agent's reaction to such cases before or by seeing 'how he goes on'. If the anger ceased immediately its cause left the room or if he can then discuss matters without any visible irritation then we have enough information to suggest that it was only a pretence of anger.

Such judgements both confirm and are explained in terms of grosser generalisations about character and it is at this level that the distinctive nature of paratactic understanding comes into play. To defend a judgement that a man is 'cool and calculating' we point to the circumstances in which he shows this aspect of his character. These circumstances are selectively emphasised. Not any display of coolness will do; indeed the careful calculation of ends hardly matters if I am playing *Scrabble* with a small child or looking up a bus timetable. It is where there is pressure upon us, in a business deal or in grand or small scale diplomacy, that these aspects of the character come into play. Such an impression of what is important is indivisible from the assessment of character traits. Indeed I find it very difficult to distinguish assessments of human character from the more general questions of morality simply because the complexity of the signals which point first one way and then another lead to an underdetermination in mental ascriptions which seems to me to invite us to make judgements about character which may or may not reveal our charitableness and humanity. More to the point, deception, dissembling, self deception and akrasia are traits which themselves have strong moral overtones. Yet I argue that their existence is required for an understanding of much behaviour even of, as I shall argue shortly, the more straightforward human behaviour.

We have moved very rapidly to questions of the estimate of relative importance. Such estimates may vary from culture to culture. A culture in which violence is commonplace and unregarded and where violence is not used deliberately as a means of securing aims might be a culture in which coolness would not be revealed in those actions where we look for it. Equally such judgements can vary from individual to individual. When a relationship goes sour, the parties often differ on their assessment of the significance of various events and episodes. What seems a trivial and uncharacteristic misdemeanour to one may seem revealingly symptomatic to the other.

To summarise, I could simply concede that the claims about selection and paratactic do not apply to some mental judgements such as those made 'straight off'. Indeed the analogy of art would be instructive here for we have to assume that we have a work of art, a painting, a text or a sculpture which exists independently of the interpretation in order for there to be something to interpret.

In the same way, we might imagine, there must be some basic features of a man's behaviour which provide a sort of factual base on which we could agree before proceeding to character assessment. But in another way the two cases are unlike. Human beings are always capable of more or less devious forms of pretence. Dismissing the possibility of pretence in these cases implies judgements about character just as much as does admitting it. So even a straightforward judgement that a man is angry may involve a counterfactual judgement that he is not dissembling. Thus although not all mental predicates require our assessment via what John Wisdom calls 'patterns in time' nevertheless even in these cases there may be a counterfactual reliance on more general and 'deeper' traits of the personality. These may reveal themselves over a long period and may not be so easily recognised; precisely such moral commitments and characteristics like selfishness or humanity require an assemblage of hints from fragments of behaviour. Children do not learn to apply ideas like self deception without some experience of life. Nice people can be taken in by devious people and sometimes find it hard to believe that their fellow human beings can be selfish or malevolent. They do not expect and do not find it. It is precisely here that the idea of the interpretation of character seems so important. It is also those aspects of behaviour which seem to us to be significant which matter in the assessment. We speak of a man as humorous but not as an ice cream eater, for example, though he might well spend as much time in a day eating ice cream as cracking jokes which make people laugh.

I have written as though there is a marked divergence between art and life here. But a case can be made for re-establishing the parallel. The words which comprise a text are not merely inscriptions; qua elements of a text as opposed to mere marks on paper they have meaning. Often, perhaps invariably, the meaning of the overall text is used to determine the meaning of its constituent parts. This is the hermeneutic circle. But although the parallels are significant, nothing compares with the role of pretence.

Our conception of a person involves the idea of a person capable of self description. It is a theme which briefly surfaced earlier in this book. The man who is weak willed both has reasons not to do what he does and, more pertinently, knows of these reasons; the self deceiver, too, could describe himself as evasive even if,

ex hypothesi, he does not do so. For both states, a necessary condition
is the possibility of so describing himself; in order that it count as self deception and not as ignorance, the counterfactual claim that he could so describe himself must hold much as must the assumption that the akratic could act differently from the way he does.

It is the possibility of self deception which leads us to the final piece in the puzzle, the role of the self image and the part played in its generation by social pressures and ideological considerations. We typically deceive ourselves over those matters in which we have a strong interest. In his discussion of Henry James's story 'The path of duty', Edmund Wilson[2] sees the main protaganist as self deceiving. The narrator is an American lady living in London who intervenes in the plans of an aristocrat who expects to succeed to a desirable title, eventually inducing him to marry a woman other than the woman he plans, all under the pretence of keeping him to the path of duty. It dawns on the reader that she is acting from *Schadenfreude* and will not admit it to herself. Her self deception is compounded in a way which will now be familiar by her suppression of her account of the episode, ostensibly to shield others but really to shield herself.

Here we have all the ingredients of what, in the first chapter, we called 'deep interpretation'. We have first of all the paratactic form of the material. All that we have is a non-continuous narrative in which fragments of conversation and behaviour are recorded. We must then select and interpret. In interpretation we supply a syntactic account which links together the various elements in the account, providing the continuity previously lacking. Finally there are important aspects of the meaning of the narrative which do not appear *en clair* in the narrative itself.

Our example from Henry James is pertinent. The narrator has a self image which she does not wish to disturb. Rather than change it, she deceives herself; her self image is an illusion. Commonly such a self image is contrasted with what might be called the 'other image', the agent as others see her. Consider another example. In Edmund Gosse's *Father and Son*,[3] Gosse recounts the story of a certain retired solicitor, a Plymouth brother like his father, who persuaded a rich old gentleman to come to live with him. On his death the old man left his considerable fortune to the solicitor rather than to the son living in South Africa for whom he had often expressed deep affection. On receipt of the legacy the solicitor began making generous donations to the work of the Lord. Gosse senior, who, as the author delightfully observes, 'preserved a delicacy and sense of honour about money which could not have been more sensitive if he had been an ungodly man', viewed the circumstances with misgivings. The son, returning from abroad, began making enquiries which confirmed these fears; it transpired that the old man had 'signed' the will by having his fingers drawn over the document whilst terminally comatose. Interestingly, the solicitor entered into penal servitude full of the joy of the Lord, confident that he has only done his duty as a Christian in preventing the legacy from coming into the hands of an ungodly man. Indeed, instead of showing any remorse, he claimed in the dock to be conscious of the Lord saying 'Well done, thou good and faithful servant'. I suppose he had the arguments.

This does not seem like self deception and it is interesting to reflect why this is so. The agents in both our stories had an interest, as I suppose we think we all have, in presenting their behaviour in the best light. But the solicitor, in the tale as told, seems to have had no inkling that there was anything wrong with his behaviour and, without such intimations, self deception can hardly be a possibility. A certain sort of innocence precludes self deception. It is hard to ascribe it to children, for instance.

Because self deception presumes a certain level of self awareness and intelligent self criticism, some important distinctions become possible. The hypocrite is conscious of the gulf between his avowed principles and his own motives or actions, but thinks such an inconsistency of little or no significance besides the advantages he obtains. At the other extreme lies the man who lives a life so unexamined that no habits of criticism have formed. Self deception is impossible if no self criticism is possible. Such a person can neither be a deceiver nor a hypocrite. Perhaps our solicitor is such a man. As Amelie Rorty remarks, 'It is only when an agent takes the unification of his traits, his thoughts and actions, as a central project that he is capable of self deception and akrasia.'[4] By the same token, false consciousness, ideological distortion or whatever we choose to call it, is possible only in a society where there is a measure of sophistication, a means of debate and a need for a ruling class to present itself to the public in a favourable light.

The agents in our two examples have a self image and quite a clear one; the solicitor sees himself as engaged in the Lord's work, for instance. The self image is often important in self deception, in as much as some pressure is required for the agent to suppress an investigation into certain aspects of his behaviour. Why should the lady not have recognised that malice was her motive in interfering in another's marriage plans? Because malice is reprehensible and nobody likes to think of themselves as malicious; the woman's ideal self image was rather that of a person who was kindly and generous; consequently she presented her behaviour to herself as keeping the man to the path of duty. Her ideal self image represents how she would like to be. The self deceiver fails to grasp the gulf between his or her actual behaviour and what he or she would like to be; there is an unreality inherent in his or her self conception and, consequently, the actual self image of the self deceiver tends to coincide with the ideal self image. Such discrepancies as there are will be minor so that the deceiver can, with a sigh, admit to being not all he ought to be, but the admissions will not involve major failings.

Since self deception is only possible where one cares deeply for and has an interest in the object, it is not surprising that it manifests itself particularly in the case of the self image. Most of us are concerned about our own integrity and self deception may involve presenting ourselves to ourselves in a better light than is warranted. So our conception of ourselves may lie midway between another's assessment and our ideal self image. Where somebody has the self image of a devout Christian, he may deceive himself into thinking that his motivation in correcting another person is love rather than malice. Once we have a gap between the actual and the ideal self image we already have the possibility of criticism. Interpretation, I have claimed, involves the thematic understanding of character or text and is to be distinguished from those forms of surface understanding involved in merely reading off the meaning of an utterance. Critical interpretation goes a step further than this. Historically the idea is connected with unmasking, with the dissolution of false consciousness and, generically, with the removal of self deception. For self deception may also reveal itself in defence mechanisms which protect a person from those sceptical arguments which militate against his or her precious beliefs. The variety of objects at which these defence mechanisms can be directed is manifold. The neutralising of these defence mechanisms is one task of critical hermeneutics. Ideally it should have, as its outcome, a change in behaviour. This is, perhaps, the moment to record one huge difference between the role of interpretation in our knowledge of persons and the role of interpretation in the understanding of art. My higher level desires cause me to act on or to refrain from acting upon my lower level desires (in whatever sense of 'cause' is appropriate). So what is revealed to me about myself in criticism may lead me to change my behaviour as a consequence. There are no parallel ways in which the product of deep interpretation affects the surface of a fiction though it will, of course, affect my experience of that work.

Can a person be without a self image? Is it required that a person have some conception of himself? The universality of the self image is elegantly pressed by the psychoanalyst Leowald in an unpublished paper:

> In a sense, every patient, and each of us, creates a personal myth about our life and past, a myth which sustains and may destroy us. The myth may change, and in analysis, where it becomes conscious, it often does change. The created life history is neither an illusion nor an invention, but gives form and meaning to our lives.

Earlier I suggested that one necessary condition of a being counting as a person is that he or she have desires of second level. The connection between having such desires of second level about the sorts of first order desires which are or are not those he or she wishes to have certainly engages with the conception of the self image. But the self image may contain more than simply a set of second level desires. It contains also a conception of the extent to which those desires are, in fact, met by the individual and, equally important, a conception of the individual's capacity to achieve them. The difference between the ideal self image and the actual self image may rest in the gap between the extent to which the agent thinks he or she satisfies the second order desires which he or she endorses. His or her actual achievement may fall short of what is reckoned to be desirable. A more modest ideal may be achievable and one can imagine an agent conceding that a very exacting ideal self image is pointless. These judgements will, of course, vary in subtlety and accuracy and it is, perhaps, plausible to suppose that the self deceiver is often constrained by a severe self image. He or she has much to live up to and failures may be too grave to be countenanced. If you regard lying with anathema, then since lying may be required through our concern for our fellow men then either such an individual, in refusing to lie, places ease of conscience above the interests of others or he deceives himself into thinking it was not a lie after all. In this way self deception is a tribute to the intensity of his moral commitment. After all, in such cases if one does not have serious moral commitments, one has no cause for self deception.

There may also be conflicts within the self image, whether ideal or actual, just as there may be inconsistencies within the ideology which is, so often, the quarry for the various elements of the self image. Of this more later on.

It is in the interplay between the ideal self image and the reform of that self image that deep interpretation finds its role. For so far, in our application of the model of interpretation to the mind we have found no parallel to the situation in the arts where a text supports a number of mutually incompatible interpretations not one of which is supported by the text to the exclusion of the others. But in 'deep interpretation' we have such a parallel. A Marxist and a Christian may take very different views of the behaviour of a particular person just as they may take different views of the processes at work in a society. This is possible in part because they take different views of what is significant in a man's behaviour. But what makes it count as 'deep' interpretation is the way in which various elements are not taken at face value. What the apparent pattern of ordinary behaviour really reveals is 'sin' or 'distance from God' to the Christian or 'alienation' to the Marxist. The religious man may be more interested in his relations with other believers at church and in the family. For many Christians the world of work is of lesser importance. Conversely, it is in a man's relations to his fellow workers, to his boss and to the productive processes that a Marxist thinks his nature is more truly revealed. There is not only a difference of selective emphasis but a difference in how the 'surface' phenomena are taken. Even if a classical economist agrees with the Marxist in his selection of what is important for the individual, he will almost certainly disagree in his understanding of those relationships. He will not view them as exploitative, for example.

On the view of both the Marxist and the Christian, the individual is liberated when he comes to view his position in the terms prescribed by the ideology. Both self image and ideal self image change. From having seen himself as, perhaps, a rational agent, the captain of his soul, the newly converted Christian sees himself as a sinner dependent on the grace of God. From having an ideal of himself as successful in his profession or as a good paterfamilias, he sees his role as an agent in the redemption of souls. More importantly, as I have just indicated, when we are able to analyse the conception embodied in that ideal self image we may find in it strains and stresses which critical interpretation both diagnoses and reforms. So one role of critical hermeneutics lies in the changing of the self conception in various ways. Internal inconsistencies can be one such motor.

Now I can imagine a critic arguing that these forms of interpretation are, to some extent at least, corrupting; they substitute for the individual understanding of persons, a universalising recipe which is supposed to offer a critical hermeneutic for every and anybody. Is this criticism simply itself a revelation of the pervasive liberal ideology which unites academics? Well, it might be that people are as a matter of fact very different and also that the existence of a theory that they are different helps to make them so different; for they, under its influence, develop just those differences.

So the idea is that although deep interpretation is important to human contact it corrupts through the way that universalising ideology and religion sets formulae for the understanding of our fellow humans. Against such an objection we can range two reponses. First, as I have just argued, these general beliefs help to make people what they are so it will not be very surprising that they fulfil the expectations the theory provides. Second, it is hard to see how we can predict and understand our fellow's behaviour if we do not have some general recipes and these theories give such handles. But no ideology or any other general theory can give us explanations for every individual case. In normal life we only elect to probe beneath the surface when behaviour is unusual or puzzling or otherwise not explicable in the usual way. But the occasion for this particular type of critical or deep interpretation is exceptional and in this respect incompatible with the tendency of most ideologies to find the same underlying pattern in all human behaviour.

It is worth a brief detour to reflect on the differences between the way 'deep hermeneutics' is defined here and the way the term is used by Jurgen Habermas.[5] I spoke earlier of the extra step involved in decoding required before interpretation can begin. The meaning of certain elements is presumed to be opaque and has to be rendered plain before we are in a position to draw a thematic conclusion. For Habermas, deep interpretation is essentially concerned with the forms of systematically distorted communication we meet in the neurotically ill and in ideologically biased communication. Language itself can be corrupted in this way, either by illness or by the desire to exercise power and authority over others. So as the neurotic patient's communications to his analyst reflect the distortions brought on by his trauma so the language of economics and politics, in particular, reflects ideological pressures. Habermas's more recent work in which he uses the linguistic model of sender–receiver rather than the Freudian model of analyst–analysand is rather further from my preoccupations.

Despite the parallel interests which unite the younger Habermas and myself, such as the common conviction that self deception is the nearest of our demotic concepts to the subject matter of both psychoanalysis and ideology, there are major differences. The idea of a systematic deformation suggests that there is an undistorted original which we recover by cancelling out the distortions. But it is central to my position that there is no right answer for either the psychoanalyst or the critic of ideology; both are interpretative systems which go beyond what the evidential basis determines. The redescription the analyst offers itself embodies selective emphases which cannot themselves be justified as being dictated by the facts. The analyst is much like a critic who presents an artist, not with a clue to the meaning of his work, but with an account of its origins. He is a historiographer *manqué* rather than a historian *manqué*. He deals in historical narratives.

It is also worth mentioning that this aspect of human behaviour is completely missed by those who make rationality a precondition of the understanding of human behaviour or of linguistic communication. What Davidson and his followers, presumably after St Augustine, call the principle of charity or humanity enshrines a misguided idea which plays little role in the actual behaviour of the anthropologist. He tolerates a measure of inconsistency and irrationality which is at odds with the straight commitment to the principle of charity. Like the rest of us, he expects irrationality and knows where to find it. Egyptian beliefs about grain and its cultivation probably did not embody inconsistencies. But beliefs which infringe on religious commitments almost invariably do at some point. Their ideas about the progress of the soul after death required the same person, the wife of the deceased, to be in different locations at the same time (and all this before she was dead). So how we understand the statements and what beliefs we accredit the believers on the basis of them will depend upon our understanding of the context.

Now, not only does the analysis of the self image require a selective emphasis in the interpretation of the character in the way I have described earlier but societies themselves are the objects of such an interpretation. We could describe an ideology as the self image of a society. Historians and sociologists are professionally concerned with the interpretation of societies taken as a whole. But the form of interpretation in which I am particularly interested is ideological. How then does this differ from other forms of understanding? The ideologue, as we shall see, protects his interpretative understanding of society so that such understanding constantly tends towards unfalsifiability. This compounds the already tenuous connection of interpretation with the factual basis; for it is a fact now familiar to us that the range of plausible interpretations may be considerable.

We began this book by reflecting upon an interpretation of Polixenes's speech in *The Winter's Tale* which speaks of man as making his nature. What we now have is the germ of an idea as to how this nature may be made; it is made through the collaboration between the self image and the ideal self image. The self image is a complex which depends both upon the agent's own idea of what sort of a person he is and other people's idea of what sort of a person he is. Part of such a self image will be generic in as much as he thinks of himself as sharing it with other people. An English intellectual has a self image which will itself incorporate the assumption that he shares typical characteristics with other members of his group. More generally he will share some though not all of the stereotypical features of an Englishman. Indeed he would be much taken aback were this not so. The conception of this shared nature and that shared nature itself normally derives from the ideology in which he partakes and about this I shall have some more to say.

For the present it is necessary to stress the role of ideology in establishing the ideal self image. A person forms a conception of himself as he would like to be, and he sees this as something he should try to attain. Christians model themselves on Christ; others perhaps model themselves on Lenin, Trotsky or Che Guevara. Sartre superbly captures the way in which a Fascist's ideal self image gradually modifies his behaviour.[6]

As a child Lucien Fleurier sees a graffito in the boy's lavatory: 'Lucien Fleurier is a big beanpole.' He shrinks, partly because he resents being defined:

> He thought 'I'm big'. He was crushed with shame: big as Barataud was small and the others laughed behind his back. It was as if someone had cast a spell over him; until then it had seemed natural to see his friends from above. But now it seemed that he had been suddenly condemned to be big for the rest of his life.

But later one of his friends strikes him as being solid and rock-like. The categorisation no longer seems a threat; he would like to be this friend, stalwart and impressive. The friend turns out to be anti-Semitic. Gradually Lucien collects some of his friend's characteristics:

> Lucien still was nostalgic: he had the impression of being only a small gelatinous transparency trembling on the seat in a cafe and the boisterous agitation of the matelots seemed absurd to him. But at other times he felt hard and heavy as a rock and he was almost happy.

He gets the reputation of being particularly tough and anti-Semitic and he sells *Action Française* outside a church:

> For more than two hours, Lucien walked up and down, his face hard. The girls coming out of mass sometimes raised beautiful frank eyes towards him; then Lucien relaxed a little and felt pure and strong; he smiled at them.

Eventually he defines himself: 'I am Lucien: somebody who can't stand Jews.'

It would be wrong to say that he pretends to be an anti-Semite. The point is that he makes himself into one by choosing a role and an identity which he admires. Perhaps it would be accurate to say that he does not really choose but does little to prevent himself from being taken over by the role. He likes to think of people saying, behind his back: 'There goes old Lucien, he really hates Jews.' The ingredients of this identity are drawn from an available identity. How graphically Sartre describes the way this process takes place.

The concept of an ideology is highly controversial and I do not want to enter into the debates now though it will be apparent that I use the conception in a broader rather than a narrower way. Recent writers have identified what have been called 'total ideologies',[7] that is belief structures which contain propositions which may be true as well as false; orthodox Marxist usage, on the other hand, takes an ideology to involve false consciousness. This is not directly implied by the wider usage. The Marxist usage is to classify as ideological only those beliefs which are false and which, of course, meet the other requirements for 'ideological'. As is suggested in what I have said earlier, my usage is very close to writers like Plamenatz who use ideological in a more inclusive sense. I believe that all persons have some 'total ideology' which at least overlaps with those of other individuals in their culture. Consequently we can define an ideology rather loosely in the following way:

1 It involves broad claims about the nature of man and his values and about the mechanisms at work in society.

2 These beliefs are constitutive of the identity of a group and play a part in the self identity of those individuals who comprise it. They think of themselves as belonging to this group and as having these beliefs.

3 These beliefs are defended by methods which involve the discounting of contrary evidence and internal inconsistencies and by *ad hoc* emendations involving speculative claims as to how critics may be mistaken.

4 They are commonly beliefs which it is in somebody's interests that they hold them though it may not be in the believer's own interests that he hold them.

As I have defined ideology, these beliefs are ripe for protection through self deception as well as in other ways. A person may think of himself as belonging to a certain group, as sharing a certain lifestyle or as a person with certain beliefs; such beliefs form part of his self image or ideal self image. Now, any adjustments in these beliefs will have repercussions. For a change may require changes in patterns of behaviour and adjustments in other beliefs. Typically these beliefs occupy some sort of key role in the general structure of his beliefs. Furthermore, a change of key beliefs may involve a change of friends and require justifying one's new beliefs to one's former associates; the whole business may be very uncomfortable and there are a number of reasons why we should try to avoid it.

So, in general, defence mechanisms may help us by giving us time to meet problems; the period of grace may give us a chance to work out answers to criticism. Of course, self deception is only one amongst such well-known patterns as self induced amnesia, the projection of our own unworthy side on to others, etc. Although in moderation these are helpful modes of adjustment, *in extremis* they indicate severe maladjustment. I suppose that most of us believe that on the whole the benefits of self deception are only benefits *faute de mieux*. We admire more wholeheartedly the man who stoically faces the worst.

Not all cases of self deception relate to one's self image in this direct and intimate way. In many cases, one may deceive oneself about a matter which, if admitted, would not be inconsistent with being the sort of person one imagines oneself to be. Howard Mounce pointed out that a man whose son is an embezzler might well deceive himself about his son's character;[8] and yet it would be surely stretching the point to insist that the reason for his self deception was that he could not admit to himself that he could be the father of an embezzler. In fact such cases of self deception may be a point in our favour; it does suggest a tendency to think well of others rather than the reverse. Only by attributing to people an egoism beyond what it would be reasonable to suppose can we turn this type of self deception into a preoccupation with one's self image; the object of our concern is different here. Lukacs remarks that 'the shaking of his [Othello's] faith in Desdemona is, at the same time, the shaking of all the foundation of his whole existence'.[9] His grasp of reality depends on certain recognisable landmarks and the removal of these devastates Othello. It is in these circumstances that self deception about another seems understandable.

The defensive manoeuvres which typify the response to an attack on a person's integrity occur when his deepest beliefs are under attack. If being a Christian or a Marxist is part of his self image, he will be reluctant to countenance criticisms of these belief systems. The more securely a certain belief is lodged in his conception of himself, in the type of person he sees himself as being, the less freely can he be sceptical or critical about that belief. Szabados uses the role of defence as the basis for distinguishing self deception from wishful thinking. In wishful thinking those mechanisms which lead to the establishing of truth and falsity are not suborned or perverted.[10] But the self deceiver protects his beliefs whether or not they are specific to himself or definitive of the ideological group to which he belongs. We fear changes here. Recall the look of terror in a person's eyes when those precious beliefs are threatened.

Now the liberal is tempted to the view that ideally we should always be prepared to reconsider our beliefs, no matter how fundamental they are. It is an article of faith. But to imagine that a man's beliefs might be so malleable is hardly credible and such a person would certainly not be admirable. We would be disagreeably surprised if a Christian who regularly practised his faith was persuaded of the unintelligibility of his ideas in five minutes flat, no matter how strong the arguments. We expect people to wrestle with these beliefs and to relinquish them only with a struggle and many regrets. As well expect a person to leave an unhappy marriage with no heartache. And what would we think of a person who was even prepared to consider cannibalism or infanticide as options? We would hardly praise his open-mindedness. The epistemological model proposed by Wittgenstein in *On Certainty* is relevant here. These beliefs occupy a similar role to my conviction that I am currently operating with two arms and legs.

Ideological commitments are shared. Nietzsche makes the point with his customary clarity and insight. 'Each of us, with the best will in the world of understanding himself as individually as possible, of "knowing himself", will always bring into consciousness the non-individual and average.'[11] Evans-Prichard remarks somewhere that when a society grows too large to be bound by tribal feeling, ideology develops to provide the glue. Certainly we define groups within society by means of the ideology they espouse, although this will only be one of the methods of identifying groups. An ideology does offer a life pattern to the young. It becomes a regulative element in maturation. The individual strives to live up to the role presented to him by the ideology which the sect espouses. Ideology is an answer to the problems of identity faced by the maturing individual as well as by society and its sub-sections.

This view of the way social processes bring about both an individual identity and a conception of that identity gives content to the Aristotelian definition of man as a social animal. In his recent study, *Liberalism and the Limits of Justice*, Michael J. Sandel[12] criticises the very narrow conception of the self that Rawls inherits from traditional liberalism. Rawls sees the individuals who comprise society as self contained atoms who make self interested decisions. Such a conception of the self is too thin to allow for the creation of the self through the sort of social influences I have been sketching in this chapter. On Rawls's conception choice and action are made on the basis of the individual's desires, some of which happen to be altruistic. Sandel distinguishes firstly an instrumental sense of community where social arrangements are simply a necessary burden, a means of obtaining private ends, secondly a sentimental conception which allows that somebody may have both benevolent and selfish aims and a third, much richer conception which holds, after Aristotle, that an individual's aims, motives and conception of his or her identity are created and defined socially. It is this third which, with Sandel, I believe gives the correct account.

Even a Humean account of benevolence makes it extraneous to the individual, a sort of happy accident, much as the occurrence of altruistic desires is a matter of fortuity. But since the identity of the individual is partly a product of ideological elements the individual both shares in the ideas of the community and yet possesses an individual identity. For the mature individual living in a pluralist culture like ours, ideologies are a smorgasbord of available plans, options and lifestyles. The community, in Sandel's words imposes 'a mode of understanding partly constitutive of its own identity'.

Once created, the identity may be revised in various ways. The function of critical hermeneutics is to force revisions both in the ideology and in the self image of those whose identity makes use of it. Consistency will be one consideration. Inconsistent elements will tend to be expunged, although these pressures are not nearly as strong as those which bear on our more everyday beliefs because of the defence mechanisms which protect ideological beliefs. It is obvious to the casual observer that inconsistencies remain in ideological, religious and metaphysical systems in a way that they do not in more ordinary beliefs. The pressure of the need for effective communication ensures that we do not commonly make assertions and immediately withdraw them by contradicting ourselves. But where the connection with ordinary beliefs and common observation is often tortuous and invariably indirect, consistency may be less easy to exact. To some extent any ideological beliefs are counter to prudence. We have a stake in beliefs which, should they turn out to be false, as they not uncommonly do, require uncomfortable reappraisal.

It is perhaps worth pointing out that I regard the process by which these beliefs come to hold the position they do as essentially negative. It is not that the causes which bring about these beliefs are different from other reasons. It is more that once they have been acquired and occupy a certain role they tend to maintain their position by defence mechanisms so that evidence which would be destructive in the case of unmotivated beliefs fails to move them. There is no such thing as 'hot' belief causation.

I have followed Sandel in seeing community as contributing elements to the identity of its members. Where I have advanced beyond his analysis is in suggesting that it is the specifically ideological ideas which contribute to the identity in this way. The belief system which we have offers a view of the world, albeit a simplified and, necessarily to that extent, a distorted one. Francis Bacon,[13] in speaking of what he called the 'Idols of the Tribe', described the human intellect as 'like a false mirror, which, receiving rays irregularly, distorts and discolours the nature of things by mixing its own nature with it'.

This gives us a hint as to how we may answer the question which should, by now, be on the lips of readers. How do we distinguish those beliefs which are constitutive of the identity of the individual from those which are, so to speak, accidental? To put it another way, how do we distinguish beliefs which are essential from those which are not? Intuitively I want to say that my belief that Marrakesh is in Morocco is not part of my identity whereas my belief in the equality of blacks and whites in terms of talents and intelligence is. To answer this we must turn to how these beliefs function in debate and discussion. Is the individual anxious to defend them? Does he or she relinquish other beliefs first? How willing is he or she to countenance objections to them? The measure of how essential these beliefs are to the identity of the believer is how easily they can be modified or given up. The more defensive the believer is, the more we will take these beliefs to be part of the identity.

Of course, it is also true that an appreciation of the strengths of other ideologies may make one more tolerant of them and more sceptical about one's own; individuals vary very greatly in the intensity of their commitment to their own ideology. But for many the consequences of this expansion of their knowledge leads to a moderate scepticism. In turn this scepticism may itself become ideological and part of their self image. Most educated Westerners see themselves as prepared to revise their opinions even if they are more reluctant to do so than they imagine.

It would be wrong to suggest that a life free of self deception and of the employment of self defensive mechanisms is possible. It is, as we have seen, very important to have an estimate of one's capabilities, and such an estimate stems from a self image, even if this is not made articulate. But the pressures of both ideology and a conception of one's own identity tend to lead to self deception. In this chapter I have tried to show that the role played by ideology in the individual self image makes self deception our fate. The ameliorating factor is that it varies in intensity.

Looking back we can now see why akrasia and self deception loomed so large in the discussion. First, these are specifically the attributes of persons; to our knowledge no other creature than *homo sapiens* displays the complexity of reflection upon and evaluation of desire which make akrasia and self deception possible. The only persons we know are members of this species. Second, of all human characteristics, these invite an explanation along the lines of 'essences'. In this book I reject the model of 'real essences' applied to persons and the human sciences. My suggestion is that man supplements his animal nature with an acquired nature which comes through a self image which contains his conception of his individual character or personality. Man has been described as the self defining animal. His nature arises in part from his self description. This is, perhaps, the truth in the existentialist denial that man has an essence. Such a created essence is a matter of influences, self assessments and acts of will. It would be grossly simplistic to say that it is created by the individual himself; he does not choose the class or society into which he is born and these are, without question, the most potent influences upon his self conception. The self image is seldom likely to be wholly accurate; we romanticise ourselves, both our merits and our failings. We are often inconsistent. But these failings are part of the conditions which make change possible. They are part of the dynamic which makes identity a matter of development rather than stasis.

What do we want to know about others, whether they are loyal, reliable, cowardly, generous and forgiving? In many ways these are backward looking. But in a crisis we say that we need to know who our friends are; they can save us. The problem is prediction. The best of friends may fail because he or she is under pressure, his children are in trouble or her mother is ill. On the whole we manage; we do predict fairly successfully. I believe that the predictions will depend upon the sort of thematic analysis which I have described here. It is certainly true that the role of generalisation varies; people vary in the degree to which they match the norm. Eccentric or intelligent people or people from unusual backgrounds may be difficult to understand and we all have friends who are perverse.

The model of science overemphasises both the possibility and the significance of predicting human behaviour. Proust, who understood human beings better than any philosopher I have ever read, is worth quoting. In M. Verdurin he presents an unpleasant bully, a man, who, as Proust says, was so jealous of his position of dominance in the little group who attended his wife's salon that he would not shrink from lying, persecution or the malicious fomentation of hatred in order to maintain his position and the cohesion of the group. Yet just after the quite appalling humiliation of the ageing homosexual Baron de Charlus by Mme Verdurin, he decides to find a place in their house for Saniette, one of their number who has lost heavily in the stock market and suffered a heart attack as a result. Saniette is a man who Verdurin has ceaselessly bullied and teased. Yet he performs this act of generosity unselfconsciously, intending to keep it from their friends. Proust concludes:

> We ought never to bear a grudge against people, ought never to judge them by some memory of an unkind action, for we do not know all the good that, at other moments, their hearts may have seriously desired and realised. And thus, from the point of view of prediction, one is mistaken. For doubtless the evil aspect which we have noted once and for all will recur; but the heart is richer than that, has many aspects which will recur also in the same person and which we refuse to acknowledge because of his previous bad behaviour.

Of Verdurin he says:

> He was a man capable of disinterestedness, of unostentatious generosity, but that does not necessarily mean a man of feeling, or a likeable man, or a scrupulous or a truthful or always a kind man. I concluded that it was as difficult to

present a fixed range of character as of societies and passions. For a character alters more than they do.

6

HOW MAN CREATED MIND

This last chapter provides the keystone and completes the argument. I have treated the human mind as though it is a human creation, claiming that the modes of understanding we think of as hermeneutic are required. The short way to a general justification for this approach is to show that we are entitled to treat the human mind as though it is a human creation precisely because it is a human creation and this surprising thesis will indeed be my conclusion. Some speculation in the form of fictive history is required but, as I shall suggest, there are familiar precedents for this in political theory. It is not unphilosophical to invent origins and my fiction is a good deal more plausible than those offered by Hobbes, Locke or Nozick to account for the origins of society. It is a history of a general and abstract sort and will stimulate some distinctively philosophical arguments about the acquisition of concepts.

In his recent book *The Renewal of Literature*, Richard Poirier[1] says that Emerson implies that language is the gift of consciousness and I suppose in this he reflects what would be the first unthought out response of most of us to the relation between the two. In this final chapter I shall argue that the relation is precisely the reverse, that consciousness (or more precisely self consciousness) is the gift of language.

When we talk about the existence of minds we might be thinking of the existence of creatures who perceive, remember or have beliefs. In that sense, of course, animals can have minds. But there is perhaps a weightier sense in which we think of minds, the sense in which Descartes speaks of minds. Creatures who have minds are self conscious. They think about themselves and reflect upon what they do and what they believe. As far as we know only human beings have minds in this sense. Some Eastern systems of thought make a sharp distinction between two sorts of mind, the minds which the more complex mammals possess and those which human beings have. It is the latter, richer concept of mind about which I want to speak here.

For anyone with a feeling for the nuances of English, there is something fishy about defining minds in terms of self consciousness; a man could be self conscious when introducing a former girl friend to his wife but unselfconscious about his exploits in sport where another man might be embarrassed to mention them. What we normally mean by self consciousness is something akin to embarrassment. Philosophers use the term in a much wider and non-demotic way, of course. Self consciousness implies reflection upon one's thoughts and actions and it denotes what is distinctive about human beings. Although it may be shown in different ways, such as the way that second order desires veto first order desires, nevertheless language does play a fairly central role. Here self consciousness requires reflexive understanding and it is how the existence of this self consciousness could have come about which was considered by Leibniz and by Heidegger after him as one of the two deepest philosophical questions, the other being why there is anything in existence at all.

The sense that there are deep and disquieting philosophical puzzles here may connect with the legacy of Cartesian dualism, the idea that the universe contains two sorts of things, minds as well as bodies, which have two distinct forms of knowledge associated with them, perception for the natural world of material bodies and introspection for the mind. The prevalence of this doctrine amongst people who are not philosophically sophisticated is testimony to the power of philosophy to filter down into ordinary conceptions of how we think about ourselves and our world.

The problems of dualism are familiar. Apart from our aesthetic preference for some form of monism, for a world with a single sort of entity in it, there are huge difficulties about the relationship between mind and matter. Clearly we learn from our encounter with the world around us and equally clearly we can change that world by what we do. So how do we explain the connections between the two? How can changes in one of these substances cause changes in another? Dualism itself does not help us to understand why there are self conscious beings in the world. All that it can offer is a sort of double act of creation whereby both matter and mind come into being. What I believe we need is an argument which will show that the existence of self consciousness is unproblematic in that it is not very surprising that self conscious beings should have evolved.

Now there is a form of explanation which has yet to be tried here. What we might call ideal historical explanations have a role in philosophy but they are most often to be found in political theory. Contract theories are of this form. They explain political obligation in terms of a hypothesised initial contract. Thus if men and women agreed at some point to give up some of their liberty in order to have safety against aggression, then we might be able to explain our obligation to obey the government in terms of our already having ceded some of our liberties in return for a government promise to protect us against the violence of our fellow human beings. We can hardly provide evidence that such a contract was made (nor can we for the narrative I offer) but the idea has been thought to play a role in helping us to understand not only the advantages of living in society but the basis of political obligation. However, if the idea of a contract is to be at all helpful then it is necessary to think that it or something quite like it happened in human history and the same goes for the sort of speculative history I offer here. It is a conjecture as to what might have happened.

If we can show that it is not surprising that self consciousness emerged, we may have an account which renders the existence of minds as unmysterious as the appearance of design in the universe, something which we now know can be explained by a Darwinian theory. Perhaps we cannot show that the development of minds is necessary but it may be enough to show it is not at all unlikely. It is not implausible to suppose that, like other human characteristics, the broad class of beliefs, emotions, motives, memories and all that is involved in self consciousness, were acquired by early *homo sapiens* or his precursors gradually over a long period. When we think of matters this way then we avoid the reification of the human mind which disfigures Cartesianism. Obviously to talk about the mind in the Cartesian way as though it is an entity or a substance is deeply antithetical to my approach; one way in which the idea of the human mind as a Cartesian substance is unsatisfactory shows in the problems of deciding at what stage a small child has a mind. If a human mind is an entity then it is either there or not. But we are all familiar with the steady development from a child's first utterances to its talking about itself, from its demanding food or drink to the clear evidence of reflection or decision. It is really quite impossible to say at what point it is clearly proper to say that the child has a mind.

So let us consider again the evolutionary fable with which I began this book. Our remote ancestors were brutish apes. But they could predict what others wanted and intended. My cat can tell whether I am going to sit indoors where she can sit on my lap or whether I am going out. She has beliefs about what I will do. Does she make decisions? This seems likely. She seems to decide whether to go in or out depending largely on Welsh weather. Now pretty evidently one ape can tell to some extent what another ape will do. A cat or an ape can tell what another cat or ape believes about the presence or absence of food. One cat seeing another about to spring knows the second cat believes there is a mouse in the grass; this will be clear if the first cat makes a pre-emptive strike for the mouse. Even if cats do not act in quite this complex way, there is little doubt that mammals higher in the evolutionary scale have done and now do. Behaviour will reveal the beliefs which can properly and sensibly be attributed. There is no problem about accrediting complex mammals with beliefs as displayed in their actions nor any problem about their beliefs about the beliefs of other animals. They do not, however, talk about their beliefs and for this reason neither they nor we have that other source of beliefs about other people which is available to us humans, namely avowals. I can tell you that I do not believe in the existence of the Yeti or of ley-lines and that I do believe that the ceolacanth can be found in the Atlantic. Once our ancestors began to describe things, a richer source of our knowledge of others became available. What a child says initially will not, of course, add much to what we could gauge from its non-linguistic behaviour but as it develops in complexity its talk becomes a significant source of information in its own right. If we think, as we should after Wittgenstein and Austin, of language as a form of behaviour, then I think it is patent that the only way gesture, for example, could become sufficiently complex and differentiated for it to be capable of expressing conditionals or subjunctives or predictions about what somebody will do tomorrow would be for the behaviour to be so complex and differentiated as to amount to the use of a language. Language use is thus not some sort of *deus ex machina* which mysteriously turned *homo sapiens* into persons but the natural outgrowth of a steadily increasing complexity in behaviour. It was not inevitable. Environment might have selectively favoured molluscs and may still come to do so. But given the environment we had it was to be expected by anybody there capable of expecting that behaviour would develop from gesture into language.

What we will describe in others and in ourselves relates, of course, to our desires, needs, intentions and, in general, to what our interests are and what we conceive of as our interests. The vocabulary of mind will, inevitably, reflect these and it is not easy to imagine that it will, in its origins, depart markedly from registering reactions and intentions. We merely have to ask ourselves what our ancestors would have wanted to use language for; the answer is surely that language would be used to request, demand, warn, etc. The need for food, affection, protection and the warning of encroaching danger are likely to be the first things language is used for. They are in the case of small children, though the child's use of language incorporates a great deal of sheer experimenting and playing with sounds and words for their own sake. Some classic studies show how the child in its second and third year experiments with various transformations and combinations of words.[2] However, it seems reasonable to suppose that historically language will initially develop where action or response are required and its early form will be to enable the speaker to present to the hearers a case for action or response. It has been well said that if we taught a chimpanzee to talk it would most likely wish to talk about bananas. Chimpanzees would not be very stimulating conversationalists. Now the initial usages are going to be intentional in form. The objects which are requested may not be present and the descriptions in which they are couched will reflect the speaker's expression of his, and his identification of others' interests. But from such beginnings we can imagine that a complex social existence will develop and lead to the proliferation of tasks, needs and interests in such a way that language both promotes and reflects this complexity. In the end we may even develop the apparently neutral causal language of natural science.

What I can recognise in others I can describe in myself and it is from this point that a mental life can develop. For I can recognise my intentions in the behaviour from which others identify my intentions and from this point on my intentions become available to me by direct inspection, so to speak. Suppose I intend to cut down a tree, for example. How do I have knowledge of what I will do? Not by observing myself in the course of doing it. Somehow my knowledge of my purposes is antecedent. Such self knowledge presumes the capacity to think and that again requires the ability to exhibit that complex behaviour which amounts to the use of a language. So a full account of how this happens will depend on the account one gives of silent thought. In brief, if I have knowledge of my aims, as opposed to those purposes which can be discerned in my action, then I must be able to formulate such knowledge either verbally or sub-verbally and in each case my knowledge depends upon my prior capacity to use language. My cat can have purposes but not knowledge of its purposes. It does not know that it intends to stalk that mouse.

Ryle's thesis that silent or private thought requires the prior existence of linguistic competence which may then be used sub-vocally is familiar enough. What we need to establish is that it is necessary that the use of a public language precedes private thought. The argument for this looks reasonably straightforward and it requires a thesis for which I shall argue at greater length in a minute. Children acquire the concepts they do in the social setting of family and school. Like any other practical skill, the use of concepts develops by trial and correction. It is consequently hard to see how anybody could acquire concepts other than through the public display of language. Once satisfactorily accomplished the skill could be employed in addressing one's alter ego; of course, sometimes you may ask a child what it is thinking and get a reply which suggests an imperfect grasp of the concepts it employs.

Could we imagine a child like the young Macaulay who was reputed to have been a late talker; his first words were said to have been at the age of three when he replied to a lady who, having seen that he had hurt himself, asked him if he felt better: 'Thank you, madam, the agony has somewhat abated.' This must be apocryphal. It would be as surprising as finding a pianist who observing carefully others playing the piano from infancy to the age of eight, suddenly strolled up to the piano and gave an asssured performance of a Chopin étude. Skills are acquired through practice and language is a skill. The analogy here is quite exact. What I am suggesting is that thoughts about beliefs and desires become possible if we have language to describe the beliefs implicit in action. In general I do not think that beliefs about people have any special priority. But for the development of the human mind they are clearly crucial and that is why they loom so large in this discussion.

Earlier I imagined how our ape-like ancestors might have described themselves. But how do they describe? If they describe the behaviour in one way rather than another, then those ways of describing become available for describing their own behaviour. Consequently what an early hominid 'thinks' about itself is dependent on what it describes in others. Now human behaviour can be described in many ways. Different societies divide up our behaviour differently and the behaviour is conceptualised in different ways. So the points of origin of a language and its associated way of thinking might differ from one society to another. In some ways this will not be arbitrary. It is natural that the Inuit have a more differentiated vocabulary for 'snowing' than we have. But such borrowings as *jeux d'esprit* or *chic* show aspects of French life which, for whatever reasons, we have not labelled in our culture. Such differences could be accidental to begin with and later become fixed in the language. One could imagine all sorts of origins. But when people classify behaviour differently they also think differently about behaviour and different peoples. Consequently different thoughts are thought by different peoples.

I shall use a final analogy to present a few thoughts on the topic which, above all, preoccupies contemporary philosophical psychology, the relationship between brain and mind. Nobody doubts that possession of a brain is a *sine qua non* for mental activity. But could there be, as a minimum, a token-token identity between the two such that although there is no general pattern of relationship between a particular thought and a brain pattern of a certain configuration such that wherever, in any single brain you encounter that pattern, you know that thought is occurring, nevertheless there is always a particular occurrent brain pattern which is identical with any particular occurrent thought. Consider music. We have the sound and the sounds can be described in terms of frequencies. If there were not those frequencies there would be no music. But there has grown up from the earliest times ways of describing music in terms of personal qualities; we describe music as calm or lively. These descriptions float free of the empirical base in the sense that no knowledge of the base is required for their accurate use. The practice of so describing music has evolved quite independently. There are large measures of agreement as to how to apply these words but then, equally, there are areas of description where people disagree and where practice tolerates and indeed encourages a measure of difference. Indeed it is one of the valued aspects of the arts that such disagreements are possible and ambiguous music is prized. There are ways of describing the broad 'regional' characteristics (to use Beardsley's term) independently of the physical basis.

My suggestion is that my thinking 'Venice is the Queen of the Italian coast' is related even more remotely to what happens in my brain than the gravity displayed in Beethoven's Heiligedangesang is related to the notes in the score. For certain sequences of notes can certainly be ruled out as expressive of gravity in music whereas no particular piece of brain circuitry can be ruled out in advance of the facts as correlated with a given thought. Equally if a painting expresses a grave demeanour it is certainly proper to say that it is that particular configuration of paint which expresses the gravity or even that it is the whole of the painting and not just a part of it which expresses gravity. We might not think that a couple of brush strokes near the top right are crucial. So if you were asked in any of these cases whether or not the two are identical you might not know what to say. As I showed in chapter one, identity requires sameness of location and there is no non-question-begging way of locating thoughts. It is not even clear whether or not the question of identity is well formed. I am not sure if I understand it.

I have argued that the origin of the human mind lies in our capacity to describe actions and that from this evolves the internalising of such descriptions of oneself. Because I can describe others, I can describe myself. Animals may be able to invite or describe actions in other animals. But self description is self consciousness in embryo and here begins the life of the mind. Even if a chimpanzee could tell another chimpanzee of the presence of a predator we would not speak of a mind. But the shadowy border between animals which we think of as having no minds and persons, which have, begins to be crossed when he can characterise himself. He can say of himself 'I am angry' where before he said this of others. But to say this, overtly or to himself, is to have the thought 'I am angry'. So self consciousness begins. The ontological and chronological priority lies in human action.

There is no gap between being able to say that I am thinking of Venice and being self conscious. A more precise way of putting this would be to say that the conditions for self consciousness and the criteria for self consciousness are identical. If I can say, of myself, that I am remembering, then we have satisfied the criteria for my being conscious of my remembering, allowing, of course, for its consistency with the other things I say and do. There is nothing more to be said. In harmony with the general anti-realism of this book I would say that there are no further deep facts about myself to which this refers and which stand as conditions for its truth. There is nothing extra or further involved so there is no possibility of a gap between my being self conscious and the satisfaction of the criteria which enable me to say of myself that I am self conscious.

The obvious rejoinder will be to say that we can programme a computer or some sort of more primitive machine to say things about itself and nobody would conclude that it is conscious. Well first, and rather obviously, there will be no behaviour with which the 'self report' coheres and that parallel will be absent. But there is another aspect of this objection to which I want to give a little more attention. Human beings acquire knowledge of language and with it they acquire concepts over a lengthy learning period. They are not acquired instantly.

Some concepts are definable in a short expression and we can learn them by rote. The terms in a technical dictionary are an example. But this is not possible for most of our 'folk psychological' concepts. They are concepts which we show we possess in the way we exhibit them in practice. They are concepts which we have to learn and use over a period of time, gradually acquiring mastery. Think of concepts like moral weakness, charm, sophistication, hypocrisy, cunning, being maladroit, tactless, etc. We cannot imagine a child using these words and knowing what it is saying. It is unthinkable that we could say that a baby is deceitful or insincere or self deceiving in its crying. I will turn again to the arts for a parallel. Could somebody be born with the capacity to play the Elgar violin concerto or acquire the capacity suddenly at sixteen? In one sense the answer must clearly be 'no'. Even if, *mirabile dictu*, such a prodigy appeared, he or she will play the notes rather than the music. The reason is that playing the Elgar is an activity that belongs to a long line of musical interpretation. Do we have a performance in the Sammons or the Menuhin tradition? Even if it sounded like one or the other, it could not count because he or she would not have learnt it from a teacher who advised him or her on the interpretative points and difficulties.

So if it is a matter of necessity that interpretative abilities are so acquired is it then a matter of necessity with respect to other concepts? To an extent the question is, I think, unimportant. For if it is an empirical truth that our abilities are acquired over time it is a very general truth indeed. Some of our concepts certainly could not be acquired instantly – think of ideas like cunning, hypocrisy or tact which are intrinsically connected with moral training – but it might also be true of the use of 'green' and its paradigms such as grass and leaves. To have the concept is to be able to apply it to a wide range of cases and knowledge of such cases is a matter of experience. Think of a very Wittgensteinian analogy! A young person may be instructed in the use of a tool but until he or she shows practical prowess we do not say that he or she knows how to use it. The analogy is not quite apt. What we have to imagine is a situation where a tool has a recognised function but that a tradesman is not master of his craft until he can use the tool in non-standard ways as well. A competent language user uses language in the standard ways. Perhaps a computer could be expected to do as much. But, and this is yet another way in which the analogy of the aesthetic is so illuminating and, I believe, central to our understanding of what human beings are, the intelligent and articulate man or woman may use it in new circumstances and non-standard ways. Not everybody can success- fully use language in these creative ways. Some of us are more gifted writers or more articulate speakers than others. Only some of us are witty and inventive in conversation. But we can appreciate these usages in others.

Well, perhaps there is an analogy. It is the mechanic who is inventive in finding solutions where he is hampered by not having the right tool or right spare part whom we admire as a good mechanic, though we also want him to get the diagnosis right and we like to have the car repaired without it going wrong in other but related ways. Still, one test of mastery is the capacity to improvise. One way of putting what I want to say would be that linguistic mastery is, *inter alia*, the capacity to improvise, to employ language in new contexts where one has not previously used it. Just how far this is from any way in which present day computers can use language must be evident.

As philosophers we tend to forget how much linguistic mastery is a matter of degree. Educationalists know all about this. Perhaps the important point for our purposes is that we can understand the language when it is used imaginatively even if we cannot compete with those poets and writers who use language at its verges. Language use is a matter of practice and practice can vary from mundane civil service prose to wit and eloquence. We understand a concept, and this expresses itself in the ability to use the cognate word, not only when we understand its central uses but also when we grasp its use outside those areas in poetic and figurative language and in other cases where a deviant use is demanded just because no accepted locution does the trick; a word has to be drafted in and used out of context.

Not only are such usages employed but they are also understood and the understanding requires a common life. Perhaps we could programme into a computer the capacity to extend imaginatively (as we would say) its uses in the way an articulate human being does. But what about that common perception of the world which makes us understand jokes, allusions, wit. When Goldsmith said that Warburton was a weak writer, Samuel Johnson replied: 'Warburton may be absurd, but he will never be weak: he flounders well.' It is hard to see how anyone could actually understand what was being said without a knowledge of what a poor swimmer does in water. A familiarity with our world is necessary. More often, of course, you need not only a knowledge of the language but an appreciation of social customs and mores. No computer and no brain, *pace* Fodor's absurd idea of mentalese, can have this sort of linguistic competence. In the case of a language embedded in the brain such that arrays of neurones represent, it is, as has been said, completely obscure how representation occurs without some human being representing x by y. Language develops in a social context and not inside brains. To do philosophy of language after Wittgenstein and not to recognise this is like trying to do natural theology after Hume's *Dialogues*. Marx said that those who do not learn from history are doomed to repeat it. How much more true it is that those who do not learn from the history of philosophy are doomed to repeat it.

It is right to think of linguistic competence as something that somebody grows up into just as he grows into understanding the institutions of religion or the power of art. There are some gifts reserved for age. We might imagine building into a computer the capacity to learn from experience, from the world and from the social world and from its own personal history, and if we were to do this then we would be getting close to the conditions under which an understanding of language is possible but we are also getting close to simulating a human being. There are still lacuna which, to my mind are crucial: the human face, the natural reactions which it registers of love, fear, hate, amusement, and the power and variety of physical gesture which we share to a greater or lesser extent with the animal world. Language grows out of that. Many of the reactions will be reactions to others' needs. Second person usages are important and philosophers often neglect them. 'Do you need a drink?' we ask the child. It is the descriptive replies to this which are an important step in the move to self consciousness. If the system of gesture was so complex and differentiated we would be bound to count it as a language. Indeed in this way we can see that there is as smooth a transition from gesture to language as there is on the arguments I present here from the acquisition of language to self consciousness. Once the form of consciousness becomes rich enough to sustain self reflection then the narrative procedures described in the earlier chapters become the appropriate means of explaining and understanding. We need creatures complex enough to reflect upon their motives and to grade them in order for them to be candidates for interpretation.

If I can describe myself in the relevant manner then we have no reason to say that I have not a mind. What, after all, does mental life amount to? It is not necessarily the silent reflection that precedes my writing this. But thought also shows in the witticism that comes to your lips without prior rehearsal or the ability to answer straight off a question about what you intend or believe or about your reactions to somebody or something. These show mental life regardless of whether silent thought occurs. We ought to remember in this context Ryle's proper criticism of the idea that intelligent speech or action requires some sort of preliminary mental performance. Some of our most intelligent remarks are said straight off and never rehearsed. We might also recall E.M. Forster's observation: 'How do I know what I think before I say it?'

What the problem shift shows, and this is its most idiosyncratic and powerful feature, is that it is through human agency that what is peculiar to the human mind comes about. We create our minds through what we do, namely talk. Our minds are our product. It is the ultimate in pulling oneself up by the bootstraps and perhaps the first example of what Adam Smith called 'the hidden hand', the way in which our actions bring about situations which we did not intend or foresee. And in as much as we are contantly revising and enlarging the way we talk about ourselves we are constantly creating our minds. Talking about ourselves reveals self consciousness and as we say new and different things about ourselves we add to the stock of the concepts which we use to describe ourselves, much as we may add to the stock of ideas which we use to interpret the world. I have already pointed out how often we say perceptive and intelligent things without having previously thought them out. We will invent new ideas, sometimes inadvertently, and often use metaphors or neologisms. We try to describe something, find we cannot do it easily, use a circumlocution and then find or invent a word which does it for us. But we can see that this comes from our use of language and our desire to make it work for us. It is because these ways of talking develop in the individual and in society through practice that we can think of a child having a mind; but we will not think of a computer which has been programmed to use the first person in its print-outs as having a mind. The computer did not learn to use language and does not progressively expand its grasp through practice. Human beings are creatures which learn. We do not arrive in the world with preprogrammed responses like ants or bees. If we had a different nature then we might be like computers, but we do not.

When as a society we expand the range and variety of our concepts it seems to me quite proper to describe this as expanding the human mind; any resistance we have to saying this is surely atavistic Cartesianism. But it is something that we do just as our ancestors amongst the higher apes gradually created mind through their development of language. So far from being distinct from the animal world, as Descartes and the Christian tradition aver, our ancestry amongst the animals is crucial to a philosophical understanding of man. The single greatest factor in philosophical enlightenment since Greek times is the Darwinian theory of evolution. In the end the mysteriousness of mind is much like the mystery of how composers create the translucent orchestral texture of Debussy and Ravel or how Rembrandt painted lace. It is a matter of a step by step progress in which these creators develop the achievements of their predecessors. We made our minds.

NOTES

1 THE PARATACTIC IMAGINATION

1 R. Dworkin, *Law's Empire*, London, Fontana, 1983, pp. 45–86.
2 Aristotle, *Poetics*, Loeb Classical Library, London, Heinemann, 1939, 451a.
3 J. Locke, *Essay on Human Understanding*, ed. A.S. Pringle-Pattison, London, Oxford University Press, 1934, BK 3, ch.vi, p. 2.
4 R. Harre and E. Madden, *Causal Powers*, Oxford, Blackwell, 1975; S. Kripke, *Naming and Necessity*, Oxford, Blackwell, 1980, Lecture III; H. Putnam, 'The meaning of "meaning"' in *Mind, Language and Reality, Philosophical Papers*, vol. 2, Cambridge, Cambridge University Press, 1975.
5 J.L. Mackie, 'Locke's anticipation of Kripke', *Analysis*, vol. 34, 1975, p. 177; see also W.L. Uzgalis, 'The anti-essentialist Locke and natural kinds', *Philosophical Quarterly*, vol. 38, 1988, pp. 330–8 for some criticism of Mackie.
6 D.F. Pears, *Motivated Irrationality*, London, Oxford University Press, 1984.
7 C.S. Lewis, *An Allegory of Love*, New York, Galaxy, 1958, pp. 117–18.
8 See G.A. Cohen, *Karl Marx's Theory of History*, Oxford, Clarendon Press, 1978, app. I, p. 330; J. Mepham, 'The theory of ideology in *Capital*' in J. Mepham and D.H. Rubin (eds), *Issues in Marxist Philosophy*, vol III, Brighton, Harvester, 1979, p. 150.
9 J.A. Fodor, *Representations*, Brighton, Harvester, 1981, pp. 168, 170.
10 D.C. Dennett, *Brainstorms*, Brighton, Harvester, 1979, pp. 122–6; D.C. Dennett, *Content and Consciousness*, London, Routledge & Kegan Paul, 1969, pp. 190, 90–6.
11 D.F. Pears, op. cit., ch. 5; D. Davidson, 'The paradoxes of irrationality', in Richard Wollheim and James Hopkins (eds), *Philosophical Essays on Freud*, Cambridge, Cambridge University Press, 1982.
12 Roy Schafer, *Language and Insight: The Sigmund Freud Lectures*, London, Yale University Press, 1978; Roy Schafer, 'Action: its place in psychoanalytic interpretation and theory', *Annual of Psychoanalysis*, vol. I, New York, Yale University Press, 1973, pp. 150–96.
13 Fodor, *Representations*, op. cit., p. 65.
14 J.A. Fodor, *Psychological Explanation*, New York, Random House, 1968, p. 121.
15 A. Kenny, 'The homunculus fallacy', in A. Kenny (ed.), *The Legacy of Wittgenstein*, Oxford, Blackwell, 1984, pp. 125ff.

16 Harre and Madden, op. cit.
17 G. Strawson, 'Realism and causation', *Philosophical Quarterly*, vol. 37, 1987, pp. 253–77.
18 D. Davidson, *Essays on Action and Events*, London, Oxford University Press, 1981, p. 9.
19 Bryn Browne alerted me to the importance of acting on whim.
20 D.F. Pears, 'How easy is akrasia', *Philosophia*, 11, 1982, pp. 33–50.
21 A good source is E. LePore and B. McCoughlin (eds), *Actions and Events: Perspectives on the Philosophy of Donald Davidson*, Oxford, Blackwell, 1985, pp. 6, 33, 43.
22 See A. Goldman, *A Theory of Human Action*, Englewood Cliffs, N.J., Prentice-Hall, 1970.
23 M. Kundera, *The Book of Laughter and Forgetting*, Harmondsworth, Pelican, 1983, p. 165.
24 Heinz Lichtenstein, 'The dilemma of human identity', *Journal of the American Psychoanalytic Association*, vol. 11, 1963, p. 216.
25 N. Holland, 'Unity, identity, text, self', *PMLA*, 90, 1975, pp. 813–22.
26 Martin Jay, *Adorno*, London, Fontana, 1983, pp. 127, 27.
27 J. Culler, *Barthes*, London, Fontana, 1983, p. 42.
28 M. Berman, *All that's Solid Melts into Thin Air*, New York, Simon & Schuster, 1982.
29 Paul Ricouer, 'The model of the text: meaningful action considered as a text', *New Literary History*, vol. 5, 1973, pp. 91–117.

2 HERMENEUTICS AND ANTI-REALISM

1 Cleanth Brooks, 'The unity of Marlowe's *Doctor Faustus*', in J.J. Lander and W.H. Auden (eds), *To Nevill Coghill from Friends*, London, Faber, 1966, pp. 109–24 and reprinted in J. Jump (ed.), *Marlowe: Doctor Faustus. Critical Essays*, London, Macmillan, 1969.
2 J.H. Hexter, *On Historians*, London, Collins, 1979, p. 50.
3 D. Davidson, 'Mental events' in *Essays on Action and Events*, London, Oxford University Press, 1980, pp. 221–2.
4 B. Vermazen, 'The intelligibility of massive error', *Philosophical Quarterly*, vol. 33, 1983, p. 73.
5 Daniel Dennett, *Content and Consciousness*, London, Routledge & Kegan Paul, 1969, ch. 1.
6 Lars Hertzberg, 'Indeterminacy of the mental', *Proc. Aristotelian Soc.*, supp., vol. LVII, 1983, p. 92.
7 See S. Blackburn, *Spreading the Word*, London, Oxford University Press, 1984, pp. 195–7.
8 Bruno Snell, *The Greek Discovery of the Mind*, New York, Harper Torchbooks, 1960, pp. 17–19.
9 E. Leach, *Lévi-Strauss*, London, Fontana, 1970, p. 13.
10 D.A. Traversi, *Shakespeare: The Last Phase*, London, Hollis & Carter, 1954, reprinted in Kenneth Muir (ed.), *The Winter's Tale. A Selection of Critical Essays*, London, Macmillan, 1969, p. 166.
11 Harry G. Frankfurt, 'Identification and externality' and T. Penelhum, 'Human nature and external desires', in A. Rorty (ed.), *Identity of Persons*, Oxford, Blackwell, 1976.

12 For example, Harry G. Frankfurt, 'The freedom of the will and the concept of a person', *Journal of Philosophy*, vol. 68, 1971, pp. 5–20.
13 *Romans* VII: 14–25.
14 P. Churchland, *Matter and Consciousness*, Cambridge, Mass., Bradford Books, 1984, p. 25.
15 D.W. Hamlyn, 'Self-knowledge', in D.W. Hamlyn (ed.), *Perception, Learning and the Self*, London, Routledge & Kegan Paul, 1983, p. 250.

3 THE IDEA OF A FOLK PSYCHOLOGY

1 Main source material is in P. Churchland, 'Eliminative materialism and the propositional attitudes', *Journal of Philosophy*, LXXVIII, 1981, pp. 68–71 in particular, though I have also used his *Scientific Realism and the Plasticity of Mind*, Cambridge, Cambridge University Press, 1979 and *Matter and Consciousness*, Cambridge, Mass., Bradford Books, 1984. The other major sources are Patricia Churchland, *Neurophilosophy*, Cambridge, Mass., Bradford Books, 1986 and S. Stich, *From Folk Psychology to Cognitive Science: The Case against Belief*, Cambridge, Mass., Bradford Books, 1983, especially ch. 10.
2 Wilfred Sellars, 'Empiricism and the philosophy of mind', *Science, Perception and Reality*', 1963, section xv.
3 K.V. Wilkes, 'Pragmatics in science and theory in common sense', *Inquiry*, 27, 1984, pp. 339–61.
4 Stich, op. cit., p. 230.
5 Stich, op. cit., p. 101.
6 P. Churchland, 'Eliminative materialism', op. cit., p. 69.

4 AKRASIA AND SELF DECEPTION

1 D. Davidson, 'How is weakness of will possible?', *Essays on Action and Events*, London, Oxford University Press, 1980; and see C.C.W Taylor, 'Plato, Hare and Davidson on akrasia', *Mind*, vol. 89, 1980, pp. 499–518.
2 David Pears, *Motivated Irrationality*, London, Oxford University Press, 1984, p. 23.
3 William Charlton, *Weakness of Will*, Oxford, Blackwell, 1988 is an honourable exception; see p. 175.
4 Davidson, op. cit., p. 31; also pp. 3–4.
5 ibid., p. 23.
6 ibid., p. 31.
7 See John Benson, 'Oughts and wants', *Proc. Aristotelian Soc.*, supp., vol. XLII, 1968, pp. 155–72.
8 A. Kenny, *Aristotle's Theory of the Will*, London, Duckworth, 1979, pp. 165–6.
9 G.E.M. Anscombe, *Intention*, Oxford, Blackwell, 1957, p. 68.
10 J.D. Mabbutt, 'Prudence', *Proc. Aristotelian Soc.*, supp., vol. XXXVI.
11 Dorothy Walsh, '"Akrasia" reconsidered', *Ethics*, 85, 1974–5.
12 Aristotle, *Ethics*, VIII, 1161b.
13 R. Demos, 'Lying to oneself', *Journal of Philosophy*, 1980, p. 588.
14 Pears, op. cit., p. 74.
15 A.R. Mele, *Irrationality*, Oxford, Oxford University Press, 1987, pp. 125–6.

16 'How easy is akrasia?', *Philosophia*, 11, 1982, pp. 33–50 and 'Motivated irrationality', *Proc. Aristotelian Soc.*, supp., vol. LVI, 1982.
17 Davidson, op. cit., p. 23.
18 Pears, *Motivated Irrationality*, *op. cit.*, p. 27.
19 ibid., p. 91.
20 ibid., 186–7.

5 ON NOT TAKING THINGS AT FACE VALUE

1 See J. Habermas, *Communication and the Evolution of Society*, London, Heinemann, 1979, chs 2 and 3.
2 Edmund Wilson, *Triple Thnkers*, Harmondsworth, Pelican, 1962, p. 142.
3 Edmund Gosse, *Father and Son*, Harmondsworth, Penguin, 1949, p. 179.
4 Amelia Rorty, 'Self-deception, akrasia and irrationality', in J. Elster (ed.), *Multiple Selves*, Cambridge, Cambridge University Press, 1986, p. 131.
5 Habermas, op. cit., p. xii.
6 In his story 'The childhood of a leader', J.-P. Sartre, *Intimacy and Other Stories*, transl. Lloyd Alexander, London, Peter Nevill, 1953. I am indebted to my former colleague, Howard Jones, both for the example and for discussion over the years about these matters.
7 See, for example, John Plamenatz, *Ideology*, London, Macmillan, 1970, ch. 1; E. Erikson, *Identity, Youth and Crisis*, London, Faber, 1968, p. 187; Nigel Harris, *Beliefs in Society*, Harmondsworth, Pelican, 1971, p. 45; Jon Elster, 'Belief, Bias and Ideology', in M. Hollis and S. Lukes (eds), *Rationality and Relativism*, Oxford, Blackwell, 1982; and Derek Wright, *Psychology of Moral Behaviour*, Harmondsworth, Pelican, 1971, ch 8.
8 H.O. Mounce, in conversation.
9 G. Lukacs, 'The intellectual physiognomy of literary characters', in R. Baxendall (ed.), *Radical Perspectives in the Arts*, Harmondsworth, Pelican, 1972, p. 98.
10 Bela Szabados, 'Self deception and wishful thinking', *Analysis*, vol. 33, 1972–3, pp. 201–5.
11 Quoted by A.C. Danto, *Nietzsche as Philosopher*, London, Macmillan, 1968, p. 121.
12 Michael J. Sandel, *Liberalism and the Limits of Justice*, Cambridge, Cambridge University Press, 1982, pp. 148–9.
13 Francis Bacon, *Novum Organum*, ed. and transl. Robert Leslie Ellis, James Spedding and John M. Robertson, London, Routledge, 1905, p. xli.

6 HOW MAN CREATED MIND

1 Richard Poirier, *The Renewal of Literature*, London, Faber, 1988, p. 96.
2 Roger Brown and Ursula Bellugi, 'Three processes in the child's acquisition of syntax', *Harvard Educational Rev.*, vol. 34, 1964, pp. 133–51.

INDEX